Issues
for
the
NEW DECADE

TODAY'S CHALLENGE,
TOMORROW'S OPPORTUNITY

Issues
for
the
NEW DECADE

TODAY'S CHALLENGE,
TOMORROW'S OPPORTUNITY

ALPHONSE F. TREZZA, Editor

A CONFERENCE SPONSORED BY THE FLORIDA
STATE UNIVERSITY SCHOOL OF LIBRARY AND
INFORMATION STUDIES AND THE CENTER
FOR PROFESSIONAL DEVELOPMENT AND
PUBLIC SERVICE

G. K. Hall & Co. • Boston, Mass.

First published 1991
by G.K. Hall & Co.
70 Lincoln Street
Boston, Massachusetts 02111

10 9 8 7 6 5 4 3 2 1

Library of Congress Cataloging-in-Publication Data

Issues for the new decade : a conference sponsored by the Florida State
    University School of Library and Information Studies and the Center
    for Professional Development and Public Service / Alphonse F.
    Trezza, editor.
        p. cm.
    Results of the Eighth Annual Library Conference, convened Mar. 11,
1990 at Florida State University, Tallahassee, Fla.
    Includes bibliographical references and index.
    ISBN 0-8161-1939-2
    1. Library science – Congresses. 2. Information science – Congresses.
I. Trezza, Alphonse F. II. Florida State University. School of Library and
Information Studies. III. Florida State University. Center for Professional
Development and Public Service. IV. Library Conference
(8th : 1990 : Florida State University)
Z672.5.I88   1991
020 – dc20   90-28391
                                                              CIP

The paper used in this publication meets the minimum requirements of
American National Standard for Information Sciences – Permanence of Paper
for Printed Library Materials. ANSI Z39.48-1984.   ∞™
MANUFACTURED IN THE UNITED STATES OF AMERICA

Contents

v

Contents

Preface

The eighth annual Library Conference convened on the campus of the Florida State University in Tallahassee on 11 March 1990. The conference was sponsored by the Florida State University School of Library and Information Studies and the Center for Professional Development and Public Service. Alphonse F. Trezza, professor, planned and coordinated the conference with the assistance and participation of the SLIS faculty and Dean F. William Summers. The theme of "Issues for the New Decade" provided a lively platform for a program directed to the investigation and discussion of preservation, the serials dilemma, the role and effectiveness of the public library, and the legislative agenda.

The proceedings were opened by Mary Pankowski, director, Center for Professional Development and Public Service. She welcomed the conference attendees and conveyed the greetings of Bernard F. Sliger, president, Florida State University.

The keynote address, entitled "Preservation, the National Perspective," was delivered by Patricia Battin, president, Commission on Preservation and Access, Washington, D.C. In 1987, when Battin took over the leadership of the commission, preservation concerns were limited to the library and archival community. Now it includes the Congress, and several government agencies and groups. Her work and dedication were recently honored by the Association of College and Research Libraries as the recipient of the Academic or Research Librarian of the Year Award.

Battin warned of chemical censorship, emphasized reformatting as the only solution for brittle books, and reminded the audience that preservation is the first duty of every librarian. She emphasized the use of collection strategies, as there is no 100 percent solution to the problem of preservation.

No one institution can do it all; only a coordinated national effort can hope to meet such a diverse set of challenges. As a catalyst for setting a national agenda she has worked with many aspects of preservation, and she described her managerial style in this way: "Do only those things that nobody else can do."

Battin supported microfilm as the logical format of storage because it has established standards, widely available portable access, lower costs than digital formats, and ease of movement from microfilm to digital formats. She stressed that the format of storage is no longer the format of use.

Among the goals she outlined were the integration of preservation into existing programs, construction of a database of preservation materials, an increase in fiscal resources, and the completion of a 500,000 master negative demonstration project by 1992.

The keynote address was an excellent indication of the quality and vision represented in the conference papers that followed.

Preservation and Disaster Planning

"Preservation Planning in Florida" was presented by John N. Depew, associate professor, School of Library and Information Studies, Florida State University. A brief history of library collections in Florida led to a description of the problems that exist in a semitropical climate: water, leaking roofs, air-conditioning systems, storms, and fires. LSCA Title III funds were obtained to develop a program to (1) alert librarians to the nature of fire and water-related disasters, (2) train Florida librarians and staff in disaster preparedness and recovery, and (3) establish a statewide recovery network. As a result of the workshops, 71 of 119 libraries completed disaster preparedness plans.

DePew emphasized that no library can be self-sufficient in planning for preservation and will need to rely on a statewide network of expertise and resources. A recently completed survey determined the preservation needs of academic libraries in Florida, the capabilities of the libraries to meet their own preservation needs, treatment that cannot be provided, and preservation services needed. Results showed 190 libraries had developed or were developing plans, and disaster assistance was listed as the libraries' top priority. A final report will include (1) an inventory for preservation needs, (2) identification of greatest needs libraries, and (3) recommendations for service.

Lisa Fox, preservation program coordinator from SOLINET in Atlanta, Georgia, addressed "Preservation–Regional and Statewide Planning." She began with the realization that we need an army of concerned citizens to solve the preservation challenge. Cooperative programs should be regionally coordinated and hooked to statewide levels. Pooled needs are very different from pooled resources, and cooperative national programs were listed as services and activities, education and training, on-site consultation, information clearinghouses, sharing trained staff, grant procurements, conservation treatment, preservation microfilming with quality control, and cooperative buying. She stressed that conservation needs often bring out problems but that preservation is so much bigger and more important. Preservation must become standard operating procedure to be successful.

Solid, practical, and insightful advice was given in "Fox's Maxims – Factors for Success":

1. Acknowledge that cooperation is an unnatural act.

2. Begin with something you care about, not something you just feel guilty about.

3. Build in plenty of short-term local payoffs.

4. It's O.K. to start small because you'll need early success.

5. Leadership is crucial; you need the ability to build coalitions.

6. Get savvy about the political process.

7. Acknowledge differences, but speak with one voice.

8. Be opportunistic.

9. Do not reinvent the wheel.

10. Vest coordinating responsibility in an appropriate organization (one that has a stable budget, paid staff, and good relations).[1]

The third paper by James R. Johnston, director of the Joliet Public Library in Joliet, Illinois, was entitled "Born in Fire: Arson, Emergency Actions, and Recovery of the Joliet Public Library."[1] It was an excellent case study of the real problems involved in recovering from a devastating disaster. Johnston noted that disaster and conservation were on opposite ends of the spectrum. He stressed the importance of documentation for insurance purpose, the need for staff communication, the value of volunteers, and the psychological aspects of disaster response. He also stressed the importance of developing, at the state level, basic guidelines for disaster planning (see the Appendix).

The preservation discussion sessions were led by Lorraine Summers, assistant state librarian at the State Library of Florida; Deana Astle, head of technical services at the R.M. Cooper Library, Clemson University, Clemson, South Carolina; and Jan Buvinger, director of the Charleston Public Library in Charleston, South Carolina.

Pressures on the Process of Scholarly Exchange

The third general session emphasized the growing stress being placed on the traditional cycle of production and consumption of scholarly information. The unprecedented increase in the production of specialized scholarly communications since World War II and the resulting inflationary fiscal strain have disrupted the once-comfortable relationship among scholars, publishers, vendors, and libraries. The three speakers provided differing perspectives of the problem as represented by libraries, publishers, and vendors.

Charles Miller, director of the Robert Manning Strozier Library at Florida State University presided over the third general session. His introduction to the serials dilemma highlighted the complexities of the problem. The presentations were extremely varied in their viewpoints and provided fuel for an active and expressive afternoon discussion session.

"The Librarian's Response and Expectations," was presented by Duane E. Webster, executive director, Association of Research Libraries, Washington, D.C. The number of serial titles being purchased has not increased, but the cost for subscriptions has an inflation rate of more than 44+ percent. Several extensive research studies have offered probable causes for this crisis in their conclusions. Included were growth in the volume of research produced, the key role of commercial publishers and market dominance, exchange fluctuations, the economics of journal publishing, and the competition for promotion, tenure, and grants. Webster defined the major challenges for librarians as (1) managing the increases; (2) assessing how the information needs and use patterns will change over the next 10-20 years; (3) shaping the production, marketing, and use of information in electronic formats; and (4) integrating new information resources and services.

Barbara Meyers, president, Meyers Consulting Services in Washington, D.C., presented the publisher's viewpoint. She objected to the statistics used by research studies, which counted titles but not pages. Scholars, administration, agents, publishers, and librarians need to retain family relationships in the quest for mutual gains and fair standards. She pointed out that the increase in research since World War II has resulted in an increase in the volume of publications and in higher prices.

The vendor's response and expectation were presented by Nancy H. Rogers, vice president and general manager of EBSCO Subscription Services in Birmingham, Alabama. She noted that inflation at 4 percent caused a 7 to 8 percent increase per title. While European titles stabilize, U.S. titles are increasing. Her company services 100 of 119 ARL libraries, and total expenditures seemed to be keeping pace, with no decline in the number of titles procured. She noted that commercial publishers are tending to publish noncommercial titles. She described the types of budget analyses that EBSCO provides in an effort to aid libraries with their fiscal planning and reminded the audience that publishers cannot determine the quality of the journal.[2]

The Role and Effectiveness of the Public Library

The divergent points of view regarding the role of the public library were presented in highly charged and admittedly strongly biased papers. The role of the public library changes drastically in response to social and demographic changes. Possible solutions for dealing with such changes were antipodal. Both practical, stock management type solutions and theoretical, process-oriented solutions were represented in the fourth general session

Ronald S. Kozlowski, director of the Miami-Dade Public Library System presided. "Conflicting Roles of the Public Library" was presented by Charles Robinson, director, Baltimore County Public Library in Towson, Maryland. Robinson concentrated on meeting public expectation as a way to repay our debt for tax support. With the goal of achieving the highest percentage of library use, he supported decentralized, branch library systems and denounced quantitative standards for public libraries. Included in his "not-so-standard Standards" were a materials budget of 20 percent (as opposed to 10-15 percent), support for central selection as a time saver, stock limitation to 200,000 items per building (to force weeding and lessen reader confusion), and an enforced five-year average retention age for most items.

Eleanor Jo Rodger, executive director, Public Library Association, American Library Association, Chicago, Illinois, presented her paper entitled "Public Library Effectiveness." Effectiveness measures, as Rodger defined them, use a rational systems approach, with circulation increase as a goal; a process based on a natural systems model to evaluate organizational equilibrium; an open systems resources model to analyze success in acquiring resources; and a demand that they meet the needs of strategic contingencies. Rodger emphasized provision of the best service to constituencies, which should include library hours to meet their needs, not the librarians' preference for working hours. She also warned against user satisfaction surveys as effectiveness measures.

The controversial issues presented by Robinson and Rodger were the focus of a combined discussion session led by Ronald Kozlowski and Sandra M. Cooper, chief, Bureau of Library Development, at the State Library of Florida.

Samuel Lazerow Memorial Lecture
The National Legislative Agenda

Dean Summers introduced Gary E. Strong, state librarian at State Library of California, in Sacramento. Mr. Strong delivered the Samuel Lazerow Memorial Lecture entitled "The National Legislative Agenda." He opened with a warning that the treasure of freedom is dependent on the survival of our libraries. To survive, we must support two arenas of the national agenda. First, we must support the retention of the LSCA resources sharing as state-based programs (not local library operation funding), and second, we must form coalitions with other organizations and institutions. Strong stressed the importance of government information being available through public access. The fact that congressional federal agencies are still in charge of the dissemination of information to an informed electorate does not automatically ensure that public access will follow. Articulating the value of libraries can influence the national agenda, which must be done for the sake of our children and their educational needs. Strong emphasized that just as library automation is a multiyear process, legislative changes on a national level will also take many years of commitment.

The Federal and State Legislative Agenda

The sixth general session, on the morning of March 14, concluded the conference. The theme of "The Legislative Agenda" was continued with presentations by Eileen D. Cooke, director, American Library Association, Washington office, and Bridget L. Lamont, director of the Illinois State Library.

Cooke's speech, entitled "Federal Legislation: Current and Developing," was a timely look at ways for librarians to keep informed about the legislative agendas. She stressed the importance of leaving no stone unturned, taking advantage of all opportunities, and using the media to get the library needs message to the forefront. Legislative agendas are dictated by a list of crises; for libraries to be included in the top ten items, we must have media exposure. She also emphasized that we must not underestimate the value of the White House Conference on Libraries and Information Services. To gain legislative attention, we must be prepared to present a powerful agenda.

"State Legislation: Current and Developing," delivered by Lamont, emphasized the continued need for research and data to support libraries' requests to legislatures. She challenged the myth that the relationship between libraries and legislation is benevolent. With funding as the most pervasive concern for legislation, she cautioned against libraries slipping through the crack when public policy issues are traditionally dealt with in a crisis setting. Lamont stresses the importance of keeping the service edge, as there is no replacement for good service. The importance of libraries was demonstrated, in one way, by the fact that when corporations move to new states or communities, one of the things they want to know about is the library.

Reports from the discussion sessions were the final presentations of the conference. Each of the reports showed how diverse and challenging the issues for the new decade are, but they also indicated how fortunate we are to have a combination of strong, talented leadership and dedicated, creative professional thinking about solutions to the problems represented in "Issues for the New Decade."

SAMANTHA K. HASTINGS
School of Library and Information Studies
Florida State University
Tallahassee, Florida

MARVIN E. POLLARD, JR.
School of Library and Information Studies
Florida State University
Tallahassee, Florida

ALPHONSE F. TREZZA
Professor
School of Library and Information Studies
Florida State University
Tallahassee, Florida

Notes

1. Lisa Fox spoke from notes, and the full text of her presentation is not available.

2. Nancy H. Rogers spoke briefly from notes, and the full text of her presentation is not available.

Acknowledgments

The conference chair is deeply appreciative of the following:

The continued support of these annual conferences by the dean, F. William Summers; the faculty; and the students of the Florida State University School of Library and Information Studies. The success of any conference depends on the quality of speakers and the effectiveness of their presentations. The papers in these proceedings attest to how well we met our goal.

The conference facilities at the FSU Center for Professional Development and Public Service and the support, patience, and understanding of the staff provided an environment that made the conference comfortable, pleasant, and distraction free.

The State Library of Florida continues to support this conference by funding attendance of its key staff with LSCA Title I funds and by funding the distribution of the conference proceedings to the public libraries in Florida.

Introduction: Preservation – The National Perspective

PATRICIA BATTIN

President
Commission on Access and Preservation
Washington, D.C.

Responsibility for the preservation of knowledge – the obligation of stewardship of our printed and documentary record – is perhaps the most highly revered tradition of librarianship. That traditional service, although long taken for granted by our society, is in great jeopardy today because of the demonstrated fragility of acid paper and the uncertain longevity of the new electronic formats. The threat of slow fires consuming from within the knowledge of our culture is a topic of immense importance to our society as well as to the rest of the world.

Librarians have a long history of supporting intellectual freedom and fighting censorship so that information can flow freely to all citizens. Although aware of the titles of books that have been banned over the years, we have been slow to respond to the frightening specter of "chemical censorship."

Every medium we have used to record the creativity of the human spirit, since we moved away from stones, is subject to deterioration. Indeed, it seems that the more sophisticated our technology becomes, the flimsier the medium we employ for storage becomes. In our fast-paced throwaway society, too often we fall into the trap of devaluing the experience of the past – of believing that the explosion of new knowledge is happening so fast that it makes the wisdom of yesterday irrelevant to tomorrow. The unprecedented four-page section included in President Bush's budget request for fiscal 1991, entitled "Preserving America's Heritage," was a welcome surprise and an encouraging sign that our social perceptions are changing:

> One might ask what "preserving America's cultural heritage" may have to do with investing in America's future. To many the connection is not obvious. But the connection is important nonetheless. To the extent that investing in the future tends to emphasize technological advances...there is a need to assure a counterbalancing attention to aesthetics values. To the extent that it implies a race through time, there is a need for a balancing appreciation of history. And to the extent that America's traditional cultural values have helped make America uniquely strong, it is important that these values be preserved – in order that they may be built upon as America continues to advance.[1]

A scholar wrote to me recently about his concern for the deterioration of books printed on acid paper since 1850. He insisted that something must be done – and done at once – for the books. It is, he said, a sobering thing to have an indispensable reference work shatter into scraps despite the gentlest handling.

Estimates vary from country to country and from library to library, but substantial data exist to corroborate individual experiences that approximately 25 percent of the world's great collections is already brittle and is turning to dust because of the alum sizing introduced into the paper-making process around 1850. The alum reacts with the moisture in the air to break down the cellulose wood fibers that give paper its structural strength. In the United States, we estimate that 80 percent of the materials in our libraries and archives is published on acid paper and will inevitably crumble. The Library of Congress alone reports that 77,000 volumes in its collections move each year from the endangered state to brittleness and thence to crumbs. The New York Public Library is currently microfilming brittle books published in the 1960s. Although alternative remedies exist for a variety of deteriorating books and cultural artifacts, reformatting is the only solution for printed materials embrittled beyond repair.

The problem can be stated in even more dramatic terms. If we were to proceed at our pre-1989 pace of an approximate – and optimistic – total of 40,000 volumes a year filmed in an uncoordinated fashion with little attention paid to duplication, it would take us 2,000 years at a cost of approximately $8 billion to film all the deteriorated volumes in our large research collections alone, which contain approximately 80 million volumes or 11 million unique items. Actually, the cost would be somewhat lower because most of the books (as well as the preservation librarians) would have turned to dust long before we could reformat them. If there was ever an argument for both cooperative action and reexamined assumptions, those figures make the case. The facts become less demoralizing if we conceive of the challenge from a cooperative perspective and with the willingness to make difficult choices.

The brittle books problem, however, is only one facet of our stewardship responsibility. Books, manuscripts, correspondence, government documents – the printed record of our civilization – are prone to a host of potential disasters from flood, fire, vermin, mold, and, of course – the reason they exist – use. We must constantly remind ourselves that although the book is an unparalleled dissemination format, it is a very fragile storage device.

We must also remember that we are responsible for prospective and retrospective preservation. Which challenge is more complex and costly? The reformatting of millions of rotting books begins to look like child's play when we contemplate the complexities involved in the archival storage of machine-readable information with its corollary of transient hardware and software access systems. Most frightening of all is the ability of technology to fill our museums, our libraries, our basements, and our attics with rapidly produced and reproduced representations of human creativity, particularly in a time of shrinking financial resources and space to properly control and maintain facilities. The sheer volume of materials published today and the potential for tomorrow, despite the never-quite-realized forecast for electronic publishing, is overwhelming. Today, for example, the American federal government produces a stack of records every four months equal to all records produced in the 124 years between George Washington and Woodrow Wilson.

Whose Problem Is It, Anyway?

Representative Major Owens (D-NY) closed his remarks at the President's Program at the January 1990 ALA meeting with these words: "Preservation is the first duty of every librarian." I would go further. If we agree that our knowledge of the past is important to our present and future, then the loss of our cultural memory is not simply a library problem; it is also a social issue of immense consequence to the survival and vitality of our society. The preservation of our cultural heritage is the responsibility of every citizen to the succeeding generation.

As librarians, we bear primary responsibility for effective leadership to ensure the successful discharge of our stewardship obligations. We must mobilize the citizenry, develop the strategies, and lead the charge. We have, in the words of the librarian of Congress, James Billington, an obligation to the moral imperative of preservation. We also have the imperative to carry out that obligation in an ethical and responsible manner. Merely acquiring and saving without proper care and maintenance do not constitute preservation.

We must also stifle the understandable tendency in times of crisis to inflate the responsibility and magnify the challenge, thus creating comforting but self-serving psychic rewards for our ability to rise to the occasion. The gentle reproach of Nina Matheson, director of the William H. Welch Medical Library, Johns Hopkins University, says it well: "I don't think there is any need to think of stewardship as an act of nobility. It is . . . an accepted, common sense act, essential to a serious educational and research enterprise, and fundamental to a free society."[2]

Responsible stewardship is the core of our profession. Responsible stewardship implies making hard choices and maintaining incredibly delicate balances among a host of conflicting priorities. We are not responsible stewards if we permit our failure to make value judgments to reduce our collections, no matter how vast, to brittle crumbs. It takes courage to commit rather than to omit, to adopt a course of action, admittedly imperfect, rather than to fail to act because we cannot do it all.

How Can the Choices Be Made?

Choice is the key word in librarianship today. We no longer have the luxury of the "one size fits all" mentality (print for everybody and every function). In an environment of constant technological change, we are often misled by the blue-sky hype of the futurists and overlook the fundamental, truly revolutionary, changes quietly occurring in our daily lives. The basic fundamental change for librarians is the fact that technology now makes it possible to generate, store, disseminate, and use information in a variety of different formats, tailored to the appropriate function. To make our managerial task even more complex, the same individual often demands different formats, depending upon the particular inquiry. No longer can we assume that scientists want journals, humanists want monographs, and reading public wants spicy novels. Everyone wants a full menu of mix-and-match options with immediate and convenient access.

More than ever, the basic responsibility of the profession of librarianship is making choices. Too long have we let the books and other printed documents rot because we couldn't create a strategy that would do it all and satisfy everybody. There is no 100 percent solution.

The making of choices now dominates the entire process of developing collection strategies and ensuring continuing access to our knowledge resources. No one institution can do it all; we need to develop a rational, cooperative national context in which local and regional decisions can be made. That is why the Commission on Preservation and Access came into existence. It provides an ordered place for existing components and supplies the elements required to fill the gaps. In a sense, the current preservation crisis serves as a real-life laboratory for libraries and archives to develop new ways of sharing and coordinating stewardship obligations.

In 1984, the Association of Research Libraries (ARL) passed a resolution urging the Council on Library Resources (CLR) to establish a *national strategy for preservation*. In its first meeting in 1984, the Committee on Preservation reached two key conclusions that were to shape the establishment of a national program and today's commission:

1. Access to what is preserved is as important as the preservation of the information itself.

2. Books would receive first priority in planning for a nationwide program.

The document *Brittle Books* became the blueprint for the nationwide preservation program and the primary initial charge to the commission. These choices were made with the knowledge that they are only a partial agenda and that a comprehensive preservation program must cover a variety of other activities and knowledge resources. The case for federal funding of a massive reformatting of deteriorating brittle books is based on the principle of nonduplication accompanied by broad access to the nation. Conservation of individual artifacts, repair of damaged or brittle volumes, and deacidification of local collections are all important components of a comprehensive preservation program and must be addressed and funded from a variety of sources. The commission, however, was organized to define the *national* role – those activities best carried out at the national and international level – and to enable local and regional organizations to make choices within that broader context.

The commission's role is one of catalyst on a national scale, articulating the issues, making the problem visible, setting the agenda, creating linkages between formerly autonomous groups all with a stake in some aspect of preservation activities, coordinating the linkages, and working to institutionalize preservation practices into the operations of existing organizations. The basic goal of the commission is to work itself out of existence.

The commission has been, and will continue to be, criticized for not carrying out everyone's specific agenda. There is a curious strain of double-think in American society: We are prone to shifting off to the "national scene" responsibilities that overwhelm our local and regional financial resources. We convince ourselves that the deep pockets of the federal government are filled with someone else's cash. And so it is with preservation. The Commission on Preservation and Access and the preservation program of the National

Endowment for the Humanities were created to perform and fund activities best suited to the national scene, with the understanding that there had to be substantial commitment of action and financial resources at the local, state, and regional levels. Carole Huxley, a member of the commission's governing body, put it this way: "Priorities for a national preservation effort will be different from any particular state's, but at both the federal and state level, agencies must play the multiple roles of planners, funders, leaders, educators, and coordinators. We have to see our work at the institutional, state and national levels as part of one major effort."[3]

What Is the National Plan?

Our society is a pluralistic one that does not respond well to solutions crafted at the top and imposed upon the populace. In an environment of constant change, setting specific goals is a limiting strategy. The commission prefers to think in terms of a national plan with broad strategic goals and the flexibility to tailor tactics as needed.

The National Endowment for the Humanities has proposed a 20-year plan for federal funding to support the following activities: the reformatting of 3 million brittle volumes; the continuation of the United States Newspapers Program; the selective preservation of special collections at humanities institutions; the support of education and training programs for preservation personnel; and a variety of activities including regional information and consultation services, state planning projects, research and development, and conferences. Within these broad goals, the endowment leadership has the flexibility to react to technological changes, the emergence of new needs, and continuing refinement of strategies, as knowledge of the problem grows with experience.

Within this context, the commission has developed a similar approach. It, too, has had to make choices. The primary guiding principle is the first rule of managerial delegation: Do only those things that no one else can do. It can't provide funding for everything. The many facets of preservation require different solutions and different funding sources at all levels. Everyone has a stake. The commission can provide visibility for the cause and work with various groups to develop sensible strategies.

The commission does *not* determine the preservation agenda for library or archive communities, for the federal government, or for the sponsoring agencies. Instead, it encourages each constituency to articulate its own goals and needs within the context of the national program, with priority levels for action. Only by clearly defining needs can it move on to developing solutions.

The commission does *not* limit solutions, options, and alternatives, although it cannot investigate every idea concurrently in the same month or even in the same year. Looking at the problem from a national perspective, it is apparent that there are a host of needs and an army of organizations are involved in some aspect of preservation. The commission's task is to provide the missing links, to set out broad program goals, and then to work to define the appropriate roles at all levels.

The commission does *not* give grants but uses its restricted funds to contract for specific research studies, demonstration projects, and the support of task forces and committees designed to provide the necessary linkages between disparate groups.

Some of the Commission's Choices

The *Brittle Books* program is now well under way with the passage of legislation providing federal funding for a 20-year program to reformat 3 million brittle books in our nation's libraries. That effort is being managed by the National Endowment for the Humanities. The commission is now working with the archives community to develop a national strategy to preserve as great a portion as possible of the endangered materials residing in public, religious, corporate, and university archives.

A central collection for preservation microfilms appears to be a cost-effective means of providing universal access to the microfilms produced with NEH funding. As the commission began to explore this possibility with a number of potential organizations in both profit sectors and nonprofit sectors, it discovered that it had very little data on the volume and location of films and of storage and access policies. A reasonably primitive survey, provided the information that by 1992, approximately 500,000 master negatives will be in the academic community and that the storage and access policies vary all over the lot! The commission plans to issue a request for proposal to interested organizations to store the master negatives and to manage the distribution services on a voluntary basis for participating libraries. The goal is to provide convenient access to the user through OCLC or RLIN with the availability of paper, microform, CD-ROM, or magnetic tape formats for a cost-recovery service fee.

In the area of technology, the commission is constantly being asked, why microfilm? The answer is that there are established international standards for microfilm; its archival potential is known; it has a production infrastructure; access to it, although generally detested by users, is widely available; and it is portable around the world. Also our society is rapidly becoming a digital one, so the commission has established a Technology Assessment Advisory Committee, chaired by Rowland Brown, former president of OCLC, to explore potential applications of the new technologies for preservation.

7

The commission has set up a number of scholarly advisory committees to assist the library profession in selecting materials to be reformatted. We can't save it all; the NEH program is funded to reformat approximately one-third of the materials believed to be embrittled beyond repair. Groups of scholars are working with the commission to think not so much about what to save but about how–how to make the right choices, how technology is changing scholarship in their disciplines, and how those changes affect their information requirements in terms of format, access, and timeliness.

The commission is exploring the educational needs for this intensified concentration on preservation obligations. These needs include the integration of the concept of stewardship into the core programs in library schools, focused programs for individuals wishing to specialize in preservation management, and workshops and continuing education courses for librarians whose responsibilities now include managerial oversight of local preservation activities.

The commission has initiated an international program to create a context for international cooperation. It began with the objective of developing a compatible machine-readable database of the records of preserved materials. That mission has expanded during the past year from the initial group of four or five western European countries to interest around the world. In a sense, the international project exemplifies the unique capability of the commission to stimulate cooperative action. Because it is, in contrast to the inherent politics of national libraries, a neutral problem-solving body unencumbered by the baggage of bibliographic imperialism, it has the capacity to bring formerly autonomous groups together to work toward a common goal. Although the first goal is a compatible database of preservation records, the next thrust is to develop cooperative reformatting projects on an international scale and to share the benefits of technology explorations and research projects.

In two important areas, the alkaline paper campaign and deacidification, the commission has supported the activities spearheaded by other organizations. Improvement in the quality of materials being produced now and into the future is a continuing commission objective.

The commission is developing initiatives to help integrate preservation into the daily lives of libraries and archives because they in the end must do the work of preservation. Developing cooperative strategies to address the needs of individual libraries and contributing national perspectives to existing library programs are two general approaches. Specifically, an ad hoc task force is designing a new course for physical plant managers to help improve environmental conditions for library and archival materials. On another front, the commission has awarded a contract to help a university library and a regional conservation center explore a new configuration for a preservation

8

program that would draw heavily on contractual services, thus minimizing the need for a large commitment to internal staff.

What Is Next?

If we are to preserve our intellectual heritage for those who follow us, we must involve every layer of our society. Much activity is going on in regional, state, and local organizations to knit this effort into a vast seamless web of successful collaboration, with each unit doing what it does best. Although we begin with broad objectives, the process, to be successful, must continually evolve as we learn to build on strengths and break down older notions of turf and territory. Whether a collection is large or small, whether an organization is a library, an archive, or a museum, everyone faces three major challenges in the next decade: the preservation of collections, the lack of space for future acquisitions, and the inadequacy of financial resources to achieve the 100 percent solution. The choices are many. The needs are diverse. The costs are high. Our resources are limited. We have an unprecedented opportunity to forge from these daunting circumstances a new and viable Information Age conception of the library in the free society. It will not be easy, but if we do it well, albeit imperfectly, we will have met successfully our primary obligation of stewardship to those who follow us.

Notes

1. Richard Darman, *The Budget for Fiscal 1991* (Washington, D.C.: Government Printing Office, 1990), 165.

2. Nina W. Matheson, *Strategic Management: Knowledge as a National Resource* (Unpublished presentation at Plenary Session I, Medical Library Association Annual Meeting, New Orleans, 23 May 1988).

3. Carole Huxley (Unpublished, untitled presentation at National Conference on the Development of Statewide Preservation Programs, Library of Congress, Washington, D.C., 1-3 March 1989).

PART 1
Preservation and Disaster Planning

Preservation Planning in Florida

JOHN N. DEPEW

Associate Professor
School of Library and Information Studies
Florida State University
Tallahassee, Florida

Florida was organized as a territory in 1822 and admitted as a state in 1845. In 1845, only one quarter of the state, the northern panhandle and Key West, was occupied. The population in 1850 was about 87,000; in 1900, it was about 529,000. Most of the population in the late 1800s and early 1900s lived in rural areas. Early in the history of the territory, Congress appropriated money for the St. Augustine road, which extended from Pensacola through Tallahassee to St. Augustine. Some of the oldest libraries in the state are in towns along or near that road, but no towns had libraries dating to the early days of their existence.[1]

The first reference to libraries in the state was that of the Florida State Library. It was legally started in 1845, authorized by the state constitution, as a place to store books and maps in the state's possession.[2] In 1855, the Secretary of State served exofficio as the librarian. Library materials were stored in any out-of-the way place in the storage rooms of the capitol building. Today the library has a multiformatted collection of almost 700,000 items, including microforms, films, and videocassettes housed in a modern well-equipped library building. It supports the Florida Library Information Network, supplying over 80 percent of the interlibrary loan requests received and has a budget of almost $19 million.[3]

The oldest public library in the state was established in St. Augustine in 1874. Today it is the St. Johns County Library, has a collection of 68,000 books, and serves over 80,000 people. The Jacksonville Library and Literary Association was first organized in 1878 and then became the Jacksonville Library Association in 1883. The library was destroyed by fire in 1901 and then "vanished" until a new building was opened with the aid of a Carnegie gift in 1905.[4] Fourteen public libraries were established during the 1880s and 1890s, but there was very little library activity across the state. In fact, in the early years of the century, the towns of Pensacola and Tampa refused Carnegie gifts. Tampa did establish a Carnegie library in 1917.[5]

By 1907, nearly every town of 1,000 or more residents had a small circulating subscription library or a public library.[6] The strengths of the subscription libraries were in fiction and government documents. These libraries continued to be organized through the 1930s, "usually by women's clubs, library associations or other organizations."[7] The movement to establish public libraries led to the decline of the subscription library after the 1930s. Today there are over 380 public libraries, including branches, serving a population of almost 13 million. These libraries have total operating expenditures of over $137 million and a book stock of about 17,548,000 volumes.

The development of libraries in higher education reflects that of the public libraries. The oldest academic library in the state is that of the University of Florida, which was founded in 1853. Florida State University was established shortly thereafter, in 1857. Rollins College and Stetson University were founded in 1885 and 1887, respectively.

By 1922, the state had 113 libraries, including colleges, universities, public libraries and subscription libraries. Their total book stock was 400,000 volumes. Five libraries had between 7,000 and 9,000 volumes. In 1935, the combined holdings of the University of Florida and the Florida State College for Women were 146,412, compared to the University of Kentucky total of 146,869 volumes, the University of North Carolina total of 245,698 volumes, and the University of Virginia total of 200,644 volumes.

Fifty-four years later, in 1989, the University of Florida had 2,701,857 volumes, and Florida State University, the successor to the Florida State College for Women, had 1,718,271 volumes. The University of Miami, founded in 1926, had 1,576,560 volumes.8 The Miami-Dade system had 2,480,180 volumes; Broward County (Fort Lauderdale) had 1,537,446 volumes; Jacksonville Public had 1,810,716 volumes; Orange County (Orlando) had 1,476,492 volumes; and Tampa-Hillsborough had 1,061,770 volumes. The Division of Library and Information Services (hereinafter referred to as the state library) had 698,857 items.[9] Libraries in Florida followed the development of libraries in other parts of the country, with one significant difference: They lagged behind by at least a generation. With the help of the state library and concerned citizens, they are trying to catch up to serve a growing and information hungry population.

As one can see from this brief history of libraries in the state, collections are young and expanding. Six of the nine universities in the state university system were founded after 1955, and four after 1962. Their libraries do not have the old and rich collections found in many institutions elsewhere in the country. Yet they do have preservation problems, caused primarily by the semitropical climate. High humidity, high temperatures, and major weather systems spawning tornadoes and hurricanes combine to create environmental situations that must be addressed to reduce damage to book stocks. In addition, a number of significant collections throughout the state must be preserved; examples are the Brazilian history and literature and the Caribbean Basin collections at the University of Florida, the Cuban history and literature collection at the University of Miami, and the Florida history collection at the state library.

The Florida Library Disaster Preparedness and Recovery Project

Until recently, neither the protection of library materials during emergencies nor their salvage after damage by fire, flood, or other causes was a high priority in Florida. Yet, perhaps more than all the states, Florida certainly needs a library disaster plan. The area is often pummeled by hurricanes, tornadoes, and severe thunderstorms; libraries are frequently damaged by water from broken air-conditioning systems, leaking roofs, and other disasters.

The state library recognized that this situation must be improved and, in 1987, awarded a grant from LSCA Title III funds to the School of Library and Information Studies at Florida State University. The funds were used to implement a statewide program designed to reduce the effects of such events, particularly those caused by water, and to establish a human resource network of librarians who can provide assistance in emergencies. Its goals were (1) to alert academic and public librarians in the state to the nature of fire- and water-related disasters, (2) to train them to prepare for and respond to emergency situations in ways that would minimize damage to collections, and (3) to establish a statewide library disaster recovery network.

These goals were met by (1) conducting a survey that gathered information about the status of disaster preparedness and alerted librarians to the need for emergency readiness, (2) holding workshops throughout the state to train librarians in disaster preparedness and response, and (3) disseminating information to the participants about workshop attendees, resources available and the role of the state library in the event of an accident or emergency. Two internationally recognized experts in library disaster preparedness and recovery, Sally Buchanan and Don Etherington, worked with the project director to design the project.

Disaster Preparedness Survey

During the spring of 1987, 196 questionnaires were sent to 81 academic libraries and 115 public libraries or library systems, including the state library. Seventy-eight academic (96.3 percent) and 105 public libraries (91.3 percent) responded, for a total of 183 libraries. The total usable return was 92.9 percent.

Almost 80 percent of the libraries did not have a disaster plan; of those that did, only 12 reported that a copy of the plan was in a staff member's home. None of the plans was written to address disaster preparedness and recovery of library materials. All were concerned primarily with building evacuation and emergency procedures for the protection of human life in the event of a fire, hurricane, or windstorm, or they addressed other problems, such as bomb threats. Most library administrators briefed their staff on their plans, but many did not inform local fire, police, and emergency preparedness officials. The answers to the questions on salvage resources, identification of irreplaceable and high-priority items in the collection, and the availability of conservation and preservation experts were very revealing. From 81 percent to almost 98 percent of these questions were answered in the negative. This was a clear indication that the plans libraries did have did not address the protection of collections.

Workshops

One hundred forty-eight staff members from 119 academic and public libraries attended a disaster preparedness workshop in his or her area. Each library director was asked to select a person who had an interest in disaster planning, who was committed to implementing the plan in his or her library, and who would act as an emergency resource person, not only for the participating library, but also for other libraries in the area. The directors were also told that the workshop was not an isolated event but the foundation of a disaster resource and support network across the state, coordinated by the state library.

The Toronto Archivists manual, *An Ounce of Prevention*, and a workbook were sent to each participant several weeks in advance of the workshops. Participants were encouraged to begin reading about disaster planning and gathering emergency preparedness information about their own libraries prior to the workshops. Two copies of the workbook were given to each participant: one for retention in the library, the other to be kept in the disaster preparedness committee chairperson's home. Participants were asked to complete as much of the workbook as possible before attending the workshop.

Six workshops were held across the state from March through May 1988. An average of 25.5 persons (representing 20.5 libraries) attended each. Altogether, almost 70 percent of the targeted libraries sent staff; 71, or 59.7 percent, submitted some form of a disaster plan by the end of August 1988.

At the end of each workshop, participants were reminded of their continuing responsibility to complete their libraries' disaster plans and send them to the project director, act as resource persons in the event of disasters in other libraries in their area, and form local networks to facilitate disaster recovery.

Results

The project goals were met:

1. Academic and public librarians in the state were alerted to the nature of fire- and water-related disasters. One hundred eighty-three libraries responded to the questionnaire. The very process of reading and answering the questions raised the level of awareness of respondents. Seventy-one of the 119 libraries they represented developed disaster plans.

2. Librarians were trained in disaster preparedness and recovery. At the conclusion of the workshops, 119 libraries had at least one trained person on their staff. Several of these libraries held training sessions for their staff and helped establish local disaster preparedness support networks.

3. A statewide library disaster recovery network was implemented. The state library designated one of its professional consultants as the coordinator for disaster recovery information and referral services and set up a complete disaster referral file. Each participating librarian was given a list of addresses and phone numbers of all participants and was informed that the division would be acting as a referral service.

4. The state library is acquiring audiovisual training materials and environmental monitoring instruments and makes them available on loan to libraries in the state. The library is investigating the

possibility of stockpiling a variety of emergency supplies and equipment for loan during emergencies.

5.   The division became a member of the Disaster Avoidance and Recovery Information Group (DARING), a group of archives, businesses, and libraries that meets to discuss disaster recovery procedures. The group is located in the Tampa area.

The success of the disaster preparedness program prompted the state library to continue promoting preservation activities throughout the state. Before any concrete proposals could be made, however, the status of preservation in the state had to be determined. Therefore, a survey of preservation needs was authorized and funded for the years 1989–90.

The Preservation Needs Survey

As in other states, almost all academic and public libraries in Florida contain deteriorating and often irreplaceable materials in their collections. Much can be done to improve the condition of these items, but the longer action is delayed to rehabilitate them and change the conditions in which they are housed and read, the sooner they will become unusable. These collections include circulating books, reference books and journals, and historical and cultural resources important to Florida's past. Many of these materials are indispensable to scholars who use them to study the state's history and to learn about current conditions and trends in the state, in the Southeast, and across the nation. All library materials, including those in popular adult, young adult, and children's collections – not just those in special collections or that are rare – need proper maintenance and housing. All are capital assets that must be maintained if they are to remain usable.

The cost of implementing the good preservation practices necessary to preserve these sometimes unique materials is often much too high, however, to be borne by a single library. The state library, therefore, is providing LSCA Title III funds to discover the extent of preservation problems in academic and public libraries in the state and to assess the libraries' capabilities of meeting those needs. A major product of the study, which began last fall, will be a set of options that could be set in place to fill in gaps that may exist in local preservation treatment programs.

The objectives of the project are to:

1.   Identify the preservation needs of individual academic and public libraries in Florida.

2. Determine the extent to which each of these institutions can meet its preservation needs.

3. Prepare a list of services necessary to support adequate preservation activities.

4. Develop an inventory of options that will solve libraries' preservation needs.

The inventory of needs and options will provide a foundation for a statewide plan to develop local, regional, and statewide programs designed to address the preservation of library materials on a comprehensive and cost-effective basis. Publication of the results will help educate decision makers, librarians, and the public about the seriousness of the physical condition of valuable (and sometimes irreplaceable) library materials and historical records. The hope is that this increased awareness will ease the creation and implementation of programs to solve these problems.

A project of this magnitude must have input from a variety of experts and professionals to ensure adequate coverage of preservation needs. An advisory committee made up of librarians from large and small academic and public libraries around the state was appointed to make recommendations and review the progress of the project.

Lisa Fox, SOLINET's Preservation Program coordinator, is the consultant in the design and analysis of the program. Her expertise in preservation has been particularly valuable in helping to design the survey instrument used to gather the information about preservation needs. Because a survey of preservation of needs library materials has never been conducted in Florida, it is difficult to determine the extent of the problem here. Other states, notably New York, have examined extensively the condition of their library and historical collections. They discovered that many of their materials are deteriorating at an alarming rate and will virtually self-destruct within a few decades. Most of the problems affecting their collections lie with books and papers published from the middle of the nineteenth century up through the 1970s – in other words, the materials that make up most of the collections in Florida's libraries. It is reasonable to believe, particularly because of Florida's hot and humid climate, that library collections here are at least as seriously deteriorated as those in other states, if not worse.

It was believed that the best way to discover the extent of the preservation problem in Florida was to conduct a combination of mail, telephone interview, and site visit surveys of the state's libraries. Therefore, a questionnaire was sent to every academic and public library, including all the branch and system libraries, listed in the *1989 Florida Library Directory with Statistics*. The mail survey was designed to identify the preservation needs of every headquarters library, branch, and departmental library listed in the directory. Each library was asked to identify the following:

1. The categories and quantities of its materials needing attention.

2. The treatment the library can provide using its own facilities, staff, and so on.

3. The treatment it cannot provide for its own materials.

4. The types of preservation services it would be willing to use if they were free or provided at a reasonable cost.

5. The preservation training status of its staff.

6. Its willingness to cooperate with other libraries in developing preservation services.

Every library unit in the directory was sent the questionnaire to avoid the problems of having headquarters or main libraries try to answer for all branches or departments in their systems, a difficult and time-consuming task at best.

After the mail survey data have been analyzed, follow-up telephone interviews and on-site visits will be conducted, as necessary, to clarify and expand the information developed during the analysis. The site visits will take place in the spring of 1990. After the information is analyzed, a list of preservation treatment options and funding possibilities will be developed, as previously noted.

As of this date, several preliminary statements can be made about preservation activities and problems:

- Ninety-seven libraries have disaster plans, and 93 additional libraries are developing such plans, for a total of 190. In addition, 13 have salvage plans in effect or in progress. So, 203 libraries have some sort of disaster preparedness, response plan, or both, either in place or in process at present, in contrast to virtually none in 1987.

- Only six libraries have collections in which 50 percent or more of the holdings were published before the mid-1800s.

- Twenty-two libraries completed preservation surveys within the last five years.

- Eleven libraries have written preservation plans, and three have them in progress.

- Four libraries have preservation laboratories. One is in a public library.

- Twelve libraries are willing to share preservation equipment with other libraries in the state.

- Eighty-two libraries need access to preservation equipment, and 66 are willing to purchase such equipment in cooperation with other libraries.

Figure 1. shows the preservation services desired most by libraries in the state. Disaster assistance is the number-one priority, followed by information and training materials. Libraries are willing to pay for disaster assistance, if necessary; fumigation; training materials; workshops; and training and treatment services, in that order. If services were free, the top priority would be information, followed by consulting, referral, a newsletter, workshop, and on-site training.

Figure 1. Florida Libraries Preservation Needs Survey – 1989 Preservation Services Desired

Service	Total	Free	At Cost	Would Not Use
Consulting	302	196	57	49
	100%	65%	19%	16%
Disaster assistance	311	105	197	9
	100%	34%	63%	3%
Fumigation	279	75	129	75
	100%	27%	46%	27%
Information	298	233	40	25
	100%	78%	13%	8%
Mass deacidification	263	61	52	150
	100%	23%	20%	57%
Newsletter	299	169	81	49
	100%	57%	27%	16%
On-line searches	280	93	40	147
	100%	33%	14%	53%
On-site training	293	148	102	43

Service	Total	Free	At Cost	Would Not Use
	100%	51%	35%	15%
Pres. microfilming	282	49	98	135
	100%	17%	35%	48%
Referral	278	169	31	78
	100%	61%	11%	28%
Training	275	52	108	115
	100%	19%	39%	42%
Training materials	301	141	129	31
	100%	47%	43%	10%
Treatment services	283	46	100	137
	100%	16%	35%	48%
Workshops	302	152	118	32
	100%	50%	39%	11%
Coordination	270	121	56	93
	100%	45%	21%	34%
Other services	27	9	6	12
	100%	33%	22%	44%

The final report of the project will include (1) an inventory of preservation needs that individual libraries cannot meet, (2) identification of libraries with the greatest needs, (3) recommendations for services that must be implemented or expanded to meet those needs, and (4) options for collectively and cooperatively meeting those needs locally, at the state level, or on a regional or national basis (for example, with National Endowment for the Humanities funding for appropriate activities).

Other Activities

Preservation activities in Florida are beginning to stir. In addition to the projects supported by LSCA Title III funds through the state library, several other activities are under way.

The SOLINET Preservation Program has supported requests for workshops from the South East Florida Library Network (SEFLIN), the Tampa Bay Library Consortium (TBLC), and other groups. Vicki Thomas Stanton, head of the serials department at the University of North Florida, is the chair of the Disaster Preparedness Consortium of northeast Florida. That group not only supports its members in emergencies but also conducts workshops on book repair. A similar group was formed in the Miami and

West Palm Beach areas. The West Coast Library Consortium (WELCO), following the leadership of Paula Biles of Manatee Community College, held a Disaster Preparedness Workshop in Sarasota in October 1989.

The University of Florida Library system has the most advanced conservation and preservation program among academic and public libraries in the state. It has a trained preservation officer, Erich Kesse, who manages a conservation laboratory, a reprographics unit, and a brittle books program. It also has a trained conservator, in addition to Mr. Kesse, and several support personnel. Mr. Kesse manages the University of Florida's participation in the Research Libraries Group "Great Collections Microfilming Project, Phase II," for which the Caribbean Basin collections are being filmed. This project is supported by an NEH grant.

The State Library of Florida maintains a document restoration laboratory, which deacidifies, encapsulates, and repairs archival and library materials. Personnel in the laboratory conduct preservation workshops for archivists, usually once a year.

The Miami-Dade Public Library system has a photographic collection of 17,500 images depicting the growth of the Miami area between the 1920s and the 1950s. It also has a large art collection. The library, with support of LSCA Title I funds from the state library, is in the process of entering the images from both of these collections onto CD-ROMs. These materials will be accessible via a microcomputer-based catalog. This imaging and indexing project will protect these valuable photographs and art works from excessive handling, while permitting wider access to the public.

Another film preservation project is being conducted by the Louis Wolfson Media History Center at the Miami-Dade Public Library. The center, with the aid of a $61,594 grant from the National Historical Publications and Records Commission (NHPRC), is preserving over 7 million feet of 16-mm news film from the archives of television station WTVJ of Miami. The film covers the period from 1949 through the early 1980s. WTVJ was the first television station to broadcast in Florida, and the sixteenth in the country. Consequently, its films cover not only Miami and South Florida news, but also many state, national, and international events. The film is cleaned, spliced, transferred to archivally correct cores, and videotaped. The original film is stored in environmentally controlled spaces, and the videotape is used by the public.

The state library, in collaboration with the University of Florida, the University of Miami, and several other research libraries in the Southeast, is applying through SOLINET for an NEH grant to support a cooperative preservation microfilming project. If the proposal is successful, several valuable research collections in the Southeast will be microfilmed, among them parts of the Latin American collections of the two Florida university libraries and all of the state library's Florida travel accounts and promotional materials collection.

The Florida Bureau of Archives and Records Management, a bureau of the state library, is participating in the National Association of Government Archives and Records Administrators (NAGARA) Preservation Planning Project Test. The project's purpose is "to provide a clear, distinctive archival preservation planning tool that archives can apply to consider facility, staff, administrative, and collection requirements to assure adequate and systematic preservation of an institution's holdings and/or information of enduring value."[10]

The Florida State Historical Records Advisory Board, appointed by the governor and administered by the Bureau of Archives and Records Management, is applying for a grant from the NHPRC for funds to support regrants funds to institutions and localities within the state or for the preservation of historical records. If the proposal is accepted, matching funds will be sought from the state legislature. The goals of this program are to help build a strong local constituency to support the care and preservation of locally maintained historical records and to help local governments and institutions develop in-house archival programs to better manage their information resources and preserve records of permanent value. Several other activities are occurring here and there around the state, but these are the most significant at present.

Time is running out. One hopes that these initiatives and the programs growing from them will help us turn the hourglass over and will give us the chance to prevent the state's cultural resources from succumbing to mold or crumbling into dust.

Notes

1. Helen Virginia Stelle, *Florida Library Survey, 1935*, (A report prepared for the Florida Library Association, Tampa, 1937, pref., 6.

2. Pamela Russell Mason, "A History of Public Library Development in Florida" (Master's thesis, University of Chicago, August 1968), 6.

3. Laura James Hodges and E. Walter Terrie, eds., *1989 Florida Library Directory with Statistics* (Tallahassee: Florida Department of State, Division of Library and Information Services, 1989), 176.

4. Stelle, 6-7.

5. George B. Utley, "Jacksonville (Fla.) Public Library," *Library Journal* 30 (November 1905): 862.

6. Joseph F. Marron, "Library Activity in Florida," *Library Journal* 48 (March 1923): 217.

7. Mason, 8.

8. *American Library Directory*, 1989/90 (New York: Bowker, 1989).

9. *1989 Florida Library Directory with Statistics*, 162, 176.

10. NAGARA Preservation Planning Project. *NAGARA Preservation Program Guide and Resources for Archives Strategic Planning*, draft (Atlanta: Georgia Department of Archives and History, 1989), i.

Born in Fire: Arson, Emergency Actions, and Recovery of the Joliet Public Library

JAMES R. JOHNSTON

Director
Joliet Public Library
Joliet, Illinois

"A disaster is an overwhelming ecological disruption occurring on a scale sufficient to require outside assistance. . . . An induced catastrophe is the category of emergency commonly associated with crisis management in the public mind. It includes arson, bombings. . . ."[1]

The firebombing of the Joliet Public Library was an "induced catastrophe" according to that crisis management definition. In comparison to the earthquakes in California and the hurricane in South Carolina, the fire damage to the Joliet Public Library is minor, although not to the people of Joliet. Illinois, Florida, New York, California, and many other states are planning for true disasters. In comparison, the recovery challenges facing Joliet are far more manageable.

If we use disaster-planning guidelines as the pattern for our library service offense, we should concentrate on three zone defenses. Disasters and catastrophes are going to happen. They usually cause havoc before we can activate our plan. As professionals, we need to plan and defend well enough to score against disaster. I propose that we use perspective, perception, and practice.

Disaster Strikes!

While deterioration and entropy slowly erode our library resources, disasters and catastrophes threaten to make our resources extinct immediately. They strike at times and in places that follow more of Murphy's laws than I find comfortable as a director. Problems of acid neutralization and the latest tactics for proactive preservation do not excite the taxpayers of Joliet or the board of trustees of the Joliet Public Library (JPL). The next round of grant applications, the next building program hurdle, the next budget presentation, and the next negotiation session with the insurance adjusters are the topics that stir the blood of every director.

I direct a medium-sized public library, when considered on a national scale. The city of Joliet is the largest in our region, with between 75,000 and 82,000 residents. JPL backs up our area library system of nearly 400,000 people as first-line support. As Bridget Lamont, the director of the Illinois State Library, will attest, Illinois will require disaster plans for future per capita grants. Planning ahead to ensure a sorely needed source of funds, I blithely assigned the drafting of our plan to JPL's coordinator of adult nonfiction services. Our professional leadership meetings had reviewed two drafts in the normal, leisurely manner, targeting staff security and emergency reactions to our increasing numbers of disruptive patrons as topics of our immediate staff seminars. In the words of Kare Anderson, "Go slow to go fast!"[2] The second draft of our disaster plan was waiting on the youth services coordinator's desk to go into the computer for revision into draft three on the afternoon of 19 April 1989.

The Scene

Joliet is the ninth largest library community in Illinois, located 43 miles southwest of the Chicago loop. Joliet's single public library facility is part of a city center that is deep into the transition from *the* retail center of the city to a commercial, banking, and office center. The building is a 1903 monumental structure of limestone, arched windows, thick interior stone walls, marble floors, and ornate quarter-sawn oak trim around the windows. Since 1875, before Custer and Sitting Bull met at Little Big Horn, the Joliet Public Library has been in business.

In fairy tales, folklore, and literature sections, the youth services collection was deep and rich. Ten years of active weeding and updating brought the science, technical, and current topics collections up to a highly used level. JPL had just completed the largest annual and monthly circulations in its 114-year history. We had at least 228,000 book items in our inventory. Nearly 11,000 records and tapes were available. Ten computers were in public service in our youth services department as the core of our computer literacy program. Our shared CLSI computer system was running well. Our public catalog had been computerized since 1980.

At 8 P.M. on the evening of 19 April 1989, I gave a presentation about the library addition plans to a group of area educators. After a grueling forty-five minutes of questions, I decided not to return the drawings and model to the library. Our regular board meeting was scheduled for the evening of Thursday, 20 April 1989. Another long day was coming tomorrow with the addition plans finally reaching completion and coming up for approval. I expected to brief my brand-new board member just prior to the meeting. In my grey pinstriped suit, I stopped to relax with friends and inquire about the upcoming softball season. In short, it was just another day at the library – a long day ending with another "selling" job, even though the audience was very supportive of the concept. As I sat down to talk to the guys, the telephone rang. "Hey, Jim! It's for you!"

"The Library Is on Fire!"

At 9:39 P.M. on the evening of 19 April 1989, a rock followed by a container of flammable liquid was thrown through the window of the Joliet Public Library youth services area. The incendiary device struck a corner of shelving in the center of the juvenile nonfiction collection, splashing across the tops, spines, and edges of the books on shelves filled to 125 percent capacity. The liquid accelerant quickly ignited the oak trim around each of three outside windows of the room. When the wood trim ignited, chairs, popular young adult books, and specialty items joined the youth services nonfiction collection from 000 to 799 in fueling the fire. Only the steel core of the paperback towers and the chair frames did not burn actively.

Outside the building, three young passersby flagged a patrol officer to report that a person in a gold Corvette had stopped in the alley and had thrown something into the library through an alley window. The patrol officer reported to dispatch at 9:44 P.M. while rolling toward the scene. He confirmed the fire alarm before stopping the squad car because flames were visible in the darkened library. The fire department responded with a full company from the station two blocks away. Fire fighters were laying hose from hydrants within two minutes. Four handheld lines were deployed. The fire fighters entered through the nearest windows and glass doors the expeditious way – crash!

Listening on a scanner, a neighbor of the library's head of adult fiction heard the initial police report and called her. Before she answered her phone, the full alarm had been turned in. My wife relayed the call to me. Dropping everything, I headed for the library. My computer operator was IN the building.

I followed an ambulance responding to the alarm from another station. Unless the Clinton Street ambulance is on a call . . . MY COMPUTER OPERATOR IS IN THE BUILDING! My heart was running faster than the car! The car was speeding! My computer operator was *the only* person I saw at first!

It Is Only Property Damage!

With my heart safely restarted, I really saw the thick black smoke pouring from the broken windows and doors and the horrid orange glow from within for the first time. Soon I noticed the various staff members, neighbors, mayor, city councilmen, city manager, reporters, and spectators gathered. Within minutes, the black smoke turned grey, then white, as the fire was struck and the spray turned to steam cooling the embers. To the sound of breaking glass, the battalion chief began ventilating the building. At a single word from the battalion chief to the fire chief to the police captain, police officers cordoned off the area.

Arson!

The immediate fire area was cordoned off awaiting the arrival of the alcohol, tobacco, and firearms (ATF) agent, the state fire marshal, the fire department arson team and the police department evidence technicians.

The fire chief escorted me into the structure to locate and test the first floor electrical panel to speed ventilation. We gingerly threw in each breaker, noting every circuit that popped and taping them out of service. Our own vent fans began to help ventilating, and a few lights came on. In few minutes of limited examination as I left the library electrical panel, my subconscious made a number of instinctive choices that my conscious mind did not recognize until the 3 A.M. TO 5:30 A.M. PAUSE IN THE INVESTIGATION.

A few designated library maintenance staff members were allowed to start recovery activities away from the fire area. We were able to cover with plastic the basement periodicals that were located immediately below the fire area. We vacuumed nearly 400 gallons of water from the marble floors before it reached another carpeted area and a tiled area filled with the general fiction collection. My computer operator was escorted to the computer room to complete a full shutdown of our computer system. Within 90 minutes of the initial fire report, our basement sump pumps began to pump out a steady stream of water. On the way out of the building, I gave the first of fifty interviews. Instinctively, I reacted to the disaster with the phrase we used for our recovery marketing campaign: "The library will bounce back!"

For the next 14 hours, ATF was in control of the immediate fire scene. They tried to locate the incendiary device and obtain a sample of the chemical accelerant from the floor. We inspected coal shovel loads of charred library materials that had once occupied the twisted ranges of shelving. City tandem dump trucks hauled the remains to the city's central services garage. At the heart of the fire, pages, bindings, and ashes were nearly all we found. A chemical sample was located. A suspect had been picked up a few blocks away. The procedure halted while the agents took the chemical sniffer to test the suspect and his vehicle and to monitor the questioning. Arson investigation resumed around 1 A.M. and continued until 3 A.M.

A glazier arrived to clear the internal transoms of suspended broken glass and secure the structure. This process (BANG! CRASH! TINKLE, TINKLE, TINKLE!!) went on until dawn. A police officer was stationed at the library to secure the arson investigation site and guard the library against a possible follow-up arson try. The possibility of a follow-up arson try sent hundreds of "why?" questions shooting around in my mind.

As soon my own mental numbness cleared, I discovered two realities of disaster response:

1. Every person connected with the library will suffer some form of shock reaction, which I would have to counteract quickly, especially my own! Our outreach librarian described it later most appropriately: "Our customers' reactions, especially those of the children, were a humbling experience. The Joliet Public Library belongs to Joliet as much as their own homes and possessions. We take care of it for them!" Every stage of reaction paralleled the sequences outlined in cancer counseling: anger, denial, rejection, resignation, acceptance.[3]

2. Every person connected with the library will want to pitch right in to fix it. The real issue became clear very quickly–What must be done?

I fell back on a set of "what to do when your mind is numb" techniques from a "previous life."

Perspective, Perception, and Practice

In the dim, distant past, I served in an Army unit commanded by a short major who waved a very large cigar and bellowed, "Perspective, perception, and practice!" at the start and finish of every officers' call. "Gentlemen, your job is not a routine job! If it were routine, some sergeant would be doing it. Your job is to be ready!" Just one short year later, I understood what he meant.

On the evening of 19 April 1989, I tasted that lesson again. I understand the meaning of perspective:

- Perspective one: It is only property damage.

- Perspective two: The whole city is watching closely.

- Perspective trhee: From my own strong negative reaction of anger and frustration, I know we need a very positive focus as a "life preserver."

To gain time (remember to "Go slow to go fast!"), I asked each of the four senior people present to bring their key staff members in at staggered times, starting with maintenance and security at 5:30 A.M. I directed my assistant to initiate the telephone tree to inform board members and the other department supervisors.

Immediate Perception

The mayor, a majority of the city council, most library board members, the city manager, the fire chief, and most of the police department leadership had been present during the fire and shortly following the striking of the fire. Radio and newspaper reporters were on the scene talking to all of us, even as the fire was being struck.

As Joliet Public Library does not operate any other service facilities, the main library had to be brought back into service as soon as possible. ("The library will bounce back!") There is no way that a deranged person tossing a firebomb into our library would be allowed to keep all our good customers from having library service. How soon can we be up and running? Before I could even begin to grasp the question, I discovered firsthand why the assess-the-damage paragraph of our disaster plan draft had bothered me. It listed a sequence of statements and questions that I could not even begin to do yet. Without answers to many questions, I outlined a plan to do the obvious, a plan that would do no further harm.

The 20th of April was a beautiful spring day, which made life easier but highlighted the smoke and soot. The smell was atrocious and did not get better with age. Initial recovery actions began in earnest at first light.

All the words in the world cannot duplicate the stress, press, frustration, and urgency of day one. This scene or one resembling it may face you one day. This is the moment. Your actions and reactions right now will make or break the library in many outside eyes.

Day One—What Happened and When

At first light, the first library security people arrived. Evidence technicians replaced the patrol officer, setting up police lines and checking identification.

At 5:10 A.M. my maintenance staff arrived. They started right to work in the lobby area and in the fiction stacks sweeping glass shards from the floor.

At 7:00 A.M. the photographer arrived. He took pictures from all the places open to him.

At 7:30 A.M. a team of city building inspectors and the library architect examined and inspected all corners of the building and found no significant structural damage.

At 7:45 A.M. the glazier removed the final overhead broken glass. The building was declared **safe**. Reglazing of the front doors began because tempered plate glass of proper size and thickness was on hand.

At 7:50 A.M. the substitute electrician arrived to trace fire damage in the popped circuits. He established temporary power to the fire site to employ higher-capacity ventilation fans and add temporary lights to the few remaining serviceable fixtures.

At 7:55 A.M. and continuing for the morning at five to ten minute intervals, the library service staff began to arrive.

At 8:00 A.M. the mayor and all the members of the city council and administration who missed the night show arrived to tour the scene.

By 8:10 A.M. there were three reporters prowling next to and behind the mayor and me as we assessed the damage. What? When? How? Why? How much?

At 8:30 A.M. the local investigative reporter literally dragged me from the building to have breakfast with a group of downtown businesspeople. He outlined the reward fund idea and a replace-the-books campaign over breakfast.

At 9:00 A.M., while I was away, active arson investigation resumed with better control by library personnel. The only recovery technique still being used was extracting visibly sound items from the three feet of charred pages, covers, spines, and twisted shelves and boxing them spine down. We were aware that it takes only 48 hours for the growth of mold to begin. We did not know exactly what the smoke particles from the heavily plastic fire (from book jackets) could do to the less damaged portions of the collection. We knew we had nearly 200,000 items to clean and preserve. It was very hard to keep many staff members from handling and contaminating the inside of the closed items shelved away from the fire.

By 9:15 A.M., despite the staggered-start request, nearly every staff member had arrived. Every one wanted to get right to work fixing up his or her area. Throughout the day, I escorted staff members on their first tour and explained the immediate tasks to small groups. The hurt and frustration built up a highly charged emotional atmosphere.

Our youth services department head, who had been with us less than one year, nearly fainted at the first sight of char and piles of the collection. She had called during the short planning period asking about coming in early. I asked her to wait until normal time. To this day, there are a few minutes she does not remember. We, the veterans of the night before, were all around her to hold her up. This was a common first reaction.

We quickly discovered that our normal organization would not do. In a quick conference, we redistributed duties. Circulation became a communication section to receive and log calls. Calls offering help and setting up media interviews were designated top priority. The youth services department became a tactical group for the screening of library material from the ruins and to reestablish control of library order. Reference became our research group to seek and secure information we could use immediately. The first task of each group was to establish and clear a working base of operations with telephones.

By 11:00 A.M. a local company specializing in fire cleanup and odor removal was commissioned to direct the immediate emergency physical cleanup. Their first immediate actions started a frenzy of activity to remove the water-soaked carpeting from the wood floors. Every item in the youth services collections had to be examined and removed from the carpeted areas. Library personnel examined and identified more than 2,600 items that were soaked but appeared whole. By Friday afternoon, 77 boxes of water-soaked, but intact, materials were ready to be frozen. Dry and whole materials were removed from the youth services area and stacked around the perimeter of the adult fiction stack area. The tiled area where we had stopped the surface water on the lobby marble floor with our water vacuums became the floor-mounted vertical stack youth services collections.

Shortly after 11:15 A.M., I remembered the presence of asbestos around the overhead pipes in the fire area and lobby. I called our testing lab immediately. Ambient air sampling began just after six o'clock.

Before noon, at the recommendation of our local cleanup expert, Mr. Eric Lundquist of Document Reprocessors was contacted and asked to come to Joliet and advise. Document Reprocessors had recently completed the Los Angeles fire cleanup. Mr. Lundquist provided very valuable assistance in the timely handling of the soaked materials and in the planning of the proper restoration and cleaning of the collection. His advice and experience base added perspective to the early gut-level decisions concerning the scale and the time needed for restoring services. He directed the reboxing of materials into boxes of a manageable size and the rental of the refrigerated trailer. We sent our water-damaged books to Document Reprocessors for freeze-drying. Eric's advice and recommendations aided our appraisal of the situation so well that his higher and very thorough bid for the full cleaning and reordering was recommended to the board for acceptance. Eric Lundquist's advice and calm were an immense help in providing answers when we sorely needed answers.

At 12:15 P.M. a quorum of board members had toured and approved on the fly the drafting of reconstruction drawings and specifications by the architect for the addition. His drawings and specifications of the 49,000 square foot addition–95 percent complete–would require addition of sprinklers and fire pull alarms according to the city inspection team. Their estimate of the damage came to more than the $200,000, which made full and immediate code compliance necessary before the first floor could be approved for occupancy.

By 12:30 P.M. the office computers were packed and sent out for a detailed cleaning. Although the offices were located a floor above the fire area, the smoke and steam had filled the locked rooms and settled over everything during the night. I had started the recovery efforts from a clipboard and out of my pocket directory and schedule. For the first two weeks, I directed the library from that clipboard.

At 1:00 P.M. the social committee brought in pizza for the staff and workers. We held an impromptu staff meeting over lunch. At that meeting, we scheduled 7:00 A.M. and 4:30 P.M. department head meetings each day until further notice. These turned out to be the best thing I did on day one. Dispensing information to the staff about who was to report for work, calming fears of total layoffs, and treating each person for shock as he or she first arrived and looked served the library well starting from these meetings.

During the pizza break, I really became aware that one of the video cameras in the library was being run by our circulation supervisor as a daily record of our activities of cleanup. This is still proving valuable in documenting the locations, numbers, and details of the fire loss to the insurance adjuster.

At 1:25 P.M. the computer company set up a complete check and cleaning of the library computer.

At 1:40 P.M. I arranged with the owner of the store across the street to occupy his vacant corner store. The youth services people needed a home. Telephones and signs were sought and arranged.

At 1:48 P.M. our insurance agent arrived accompanied by a local insurance adjuster. By midday Friday, the local adjuster had been replaced by a "big time" Chicago adjuster of the same firm. Our initial estimate of the damage ranged from $600,000 to $1.2 million. The presence of the Chicago-based adjuster made the city manager and me look toward the higher figure.

Many local businesspeople came or called to advise for and against hiring a public adjuster or trusting the company. At the recommendation of the city manager, the board president, and the lieutenant governor, the Joliet Public Library hired a public adjuster. The board felt it needed the "professional insurance" of our own adjuster to assemble and document the claim and to buffer us against the inevitable "you could have done better" comments.

At 2:30 P.M. I was summoned to the newspaper offices, where the editor had called a meeting of the bankers, police chief, and city management to establish a reward fund.

USA Today and *Newsweek* were due to arrive Monday or Tuesday. The police investigation discovered a hidden security camera on the savings and loan across the alley. One picture showed a Corvette and a figure with a burning object facing the library window at approximately 9:39 P.M. The suspect from the night before was formally charged. With the arraignment, national media attention evaporated.

At 4:30 P.M. I called a halt for the day. The social committee added coffee and doughnuts and most people stayed through until 6:00 P.M.. We held our first department head conference in the lobby with everyone buzzing around us. The scope of cleanup for each individual book and area was fully realized as the local cleanup expert recommended full professional care to ensure the proper life extension of the heavily and lightly smoke damaged volumes. He used a few examples to demonstrate the why and how to us. The local emergency cleanup crew worked until dark. Pittsburgh Testing Labs set up their air-testing equipment at 6:00. At 8:15, I left the building for the day. We had lived through day one.

From Ashes to Annex

Reglazing paid morale dividends immediately. Restoration of natural light demonstrated our response to the passing public—we were coming back.

More than 800 calls were handled in the first three days after the fire. Many were from public adjusters, restoration companies, lawyers, and fire contractors. The rest were from surrounding libraries offering help, from friends volunteering to help, and from every media representative under the sun. There were so many calls that the working telephones were jammed.

All the major network television stations from Chicago, many regional radio stations, newspapers, and some magazines began calling and arriving for interviews and pictures. Because I recognized the precarious addition situation best, I decided to be the public information officer as well as the director. I tried to be as professional and businesslike as possible for each interview, especially for the various television stations. The emotions came through anyway. From moment to moment, I was forced to examine each of our activities. I relied on a critical path and key time version of supervision. If a process or sequence of actions was out of the ordinary, I tried to appear on the scene at critical places and times.

I started in that grey pinstriped suit and kept zooming down to the restroom for the famous quick change into the "grubbies" a neighbor brought to me from home for the heavy work. With so many media interviews, the art of the quick change became even quicker. The library's image and professionalism were tremendous boosts for each tired smoky staff member to view on the news. Once my youth services librarian had recovered her emotional balance, we split the interviews. Hearing her perspective when expressed to the media kept both our points of view in synchronization at a critical time. Worried whether I was in the way of my own chain of command, I asked the section leaders and key people for their reaction. Their comments to me were enlightening: "We needed to see you there. We needed that support and frequent visits. We even needed your rotten jokes!" I found that I needed their support and balance at least as much!

Colonel Jack Stephens, a professor of military science in the Notre Dame Army ROTC program a long time ago, also made an important contribution to my disaster response in the area of image. "The commander can be scared green. You are human! Just don't look like it. Your people need to know that you are with them and know that you trust them to do their jobs. Do yours: LEAD! DIRECT! ADAPT! OVERCOME! One more rifleman will rarely be decisive. An effective commander does best what he has been trained to do. Be decisive! If you're wrong, you can refocus. If you're right, you're already started. Just do not appear uncertain!" I can tell you how uncertain I felt. The staff all knew deep down that I was "in deep," but the needed morale boost still worked.

To apply all our skills to the recovery, we restructured the organization on the fly again into a communications section, a research section, a physical recovery and verification section, and the "command" group—whose real function was to direct traffic and smooth rough spots. At critical points, we made certain that we discussed the future and emphasized the contribution of each activity toward service restoration. Despite the press coverage, only the library staff members fully recognized the whole tragedy. Many of our customers still visited, and they regaled us with their favorite fire, flood and disaster stories. The pastor of the Episcopal Church across the street kept finding me to tell me his favorite stories about the value of humor and the need to air frustrations. Sadly, he had not yet installed the padded scream room in his church. While sifting through the ashes of the collection they had spent so long keeping in order and in good repair, the staff invented off-the-wall things to present to me, a "Hang in there" T-shirt, a customized epithet descriptive of our situation, and a collection of numerous strange greeting cards, the kind we all see and laugh about in stores, but rarely purchase. The mutual support and dedication of the staff warmed my heart. On the afternoon of 19 April 1989, I thought I knew our 60 people. I have come to know them better. They are both better and worse than I imagined. I am so proud of their hard work that I could burst. Because of the people who kept wading into the ashes to restore our service, Joliet Public Library services bounced back faster than the most optimistic city administration people could believe.

The state library conservation officer toured on Saturday afternoon, 22 April 1989, offering advice on recovery and preservation options. The state library staff quickly drafted a collection development grant on our behalf for $10,000 to restart a "homework" collection. Youth services morale needed that boost. Worried about cash flow, my morale needed the boost, too.

A young lady from the junior high, which had been firebombed one month before, began a drive to replace the books. She asked her classmates to donate a book that they would read. A local paperback exchange offered to collect donations (and to donate copies of any of their backroom stock) on the far side of town. Youth services set up and carried out from the middle of April through the end of May a campaign for donations. Handouts and fact sheets, featuring the newspaper headline, "LIBRARY FIREBOMBED! THE CITY ASKS WHY?", were quickly made up and distributed at local businesses. Outreach activities continued on schedule. The children were all interested in the fate of the goldfish and their seeds-to-beans projects. The news was both good and bad: the goldfish survived; the sprouts cooked!

By the 29th of April, a local radio station had planned and executed a radiothon for the library, receiving pledges of more than $15,000. The secretary of state of Illinois, Jim Edgar, called and pledged. Board and staff members helped man the phones, answering questions as well as recording donations. Many local businesses donated incentives and services as prizes.

Each community financial institution started an account for the Replace the Books Fund donations. Joliet people and our neighbors, individuals, groups, businesses, and libraries contributed over $40,000 in the first 30 days. The youth services staff and the support services staff were asked to focus on collection reestablishment even before they were finished being shocked. We set the homework collection as our top priority, aimed at the topics we knew would be assigned: science fair projects, leaves, reptiles, animals, and fourteen others. We tooled up support services to handle the heavier load of regular purchases and the fire restoration of youth factual materials.

We offered an extended amnesty period. We had no working cash register yet. We had nowhere to put returned books. We had located the bank books, but the area was sealed for three days while two deodorization processes were used.

Every loss boils down to a set of numbers and endless lists for the purpose of proving the loss. The JPL firebombing insurance claim documents the following selected highlights of loss:

22,671 books (17,400 from J nonfiction)
1,748 records
110 films
76 video cassettes
254 computer programs
184 audio cassettes
330 framed art prints
15 original works of art
2,200 books returned from Document Reprocessors after freeze-
    drying were verified for the insurance claim
84 sections of shelving
10 computers (all interior components itemized)
6 printers
56 chairs
7 computer terminals
8 tables
3 paperback towers
3 cassette players
3 carrels
And much, much more!
$235,129 in building repairs
$858,000 in valuable papers, art floater, and EDP coverage
 $121,000 in furniture and contents, including cleaning

To document the loss, we initiated a complete inventory check after the computer was ruled healthy. Using the method another Illinois library had used for its flood inventory, we verified every item in the J, E, and Y call numbers by printing them out and checking every shelf list item out to "fire" using help from all our surrounding libraries; then, when cleaning was complete, each item reshelved in our rented facility was checked in.

As soon as the Restoration Company (a division of M. F. Bank from Norcross, Georgia) was contracted to perform the demolition, bulk cleaning, and soot setting operations, the staff met to set our priorities. We were beginning to have longer-term answers. The insurance settlement would take at least six months of negotiating. The redefinition of the addition bonds to include fire reconstruction and code compliances needed to reoccupy the main library would require at least six months. Actual reconstruction work would take a minimum of three months.

The Restoration Company was charged with the reopening of the lightly damaged second floor by 6 May 1989. Our students could not be left without information during the end of term paper time. Our second floor houses all our adult nonfiction, reference, and periodical services. It would be a separate floor in terms of entrance if we reconfigured the lobby and installed a circulation desk. Power, computer cables, and telephones were sought immediately. We had to be open and running for youth services prior to 9 June 1989, the long-planned signup day for the critical summer reading program. All the promotional materials had gone out long since.

Computer terminal gear to replace the fire losses was fortunately present in their sealed shipping boxes during the fire. We had purchased it for the new addition early to take advantage of a bulk price and lower operating costs. We located a circulation desk from the closed East High School Library.

A floor plan for a 1982 adaptive reuse of a structure of 8,000 square feet was brought back to light and dusted off. I began to hunt for space to use it! There are two such structures adjacent to the library. One is vacant and one is occupied. I toured both. One was "at grade" for accessibility and had enough electric power distribution for our purposes. I swallowed my pride as I contacted the real estate agent who had caused the library months of delay with his press release about an adaptive reuse of the vacant commercial building. It would not work for an addition because of its kitty-corner location at the far northeast corner of the block of which the library owns the south half. The months of debate and the studies of materials and load capability became valuable. The most valuable items turned out to be the thought-experiment operational plans, which we had prepared to test the site's viability. It was a terrible addition, but a firebomb had changed the game to include the idea of a separate annex. All the site committee studies became very valuable for wildly different reasons than their intended purpose. The library possessed drawings and floor plans with a complete quick structural analysis of every surrounding building.

I was never so glad that the library had responded carefully and in a clear precise manner to a critic. Suddenly, I was negotiating a lease for the property rejected months before. We leased the first floor and mezzanine of an old department store, located down the alley from the library. By 12 May 1989, the library was moving boxes of cleaned and deodorized adult fiction books, all new books, all returns from circulation, and all surviving youth books into the annex.

We scheduled a volunteer moving project for Saturday, May 20, 1989. A very flexible plan for separate teams with related but separate missions was devised to accommodate from 40 to the 150 people who responded yes to our call. On the afternoon of 15 May 1989, while I was signing the lease, we had a major short circuit and a fire in a high voltage junction box in the annex. We postponed the move while electricians and city inspectors combed the structure. The local fire cleanup expert received his second job from us in fully cleaning the annex. His techniques restored the neglected, stained, and now sooted carpet to amazing cleanliness.

As soon as the carpet dried, we moved in boxes of books. The plan was to duct tape the boxes in stacks three high to form temporary shelving. After just two days, the supposedly heavy duty boxes sagged so badly that we delayed the move until Saturday, 27 May 1989. We reassembled all the salvageable shelving from the youth services department. We moved 17 sections of display shelving into the annex. The closest B. Dalton bookstore had donated them when they remodeled. We were directed to the other area B. Dalton for 28 additional sections of donated shelves from their remodeling. The shelves were different colors but designed for the 75 pound per square foot loading of a commercial structure.

On the bright sunny morning of Saturday, 27 May 1989, more than 116 volunteers appeared (116 signed in; more worked) with 58 staff members. Every staff member was presented a "Joliet Public Library Bounces Back" T-shirt for identification. Every volunteer received a button with the same logo, all donated by the Friends of the Library group and produced at cost by a local T-shirt shop. Pizza by Marchelloni donated pizza to all buttoned and T-shirted people from their mobile pizza truck. McDonalds and Kemmerer Bottling (the local Seven-Up bottler and distributor) donated the drinks. Dunkin Donut and Home Cut Donuts supplied dessert. Local radio stations did interviews and live broadcasts. Joliet Warehouse and Transfer, the local Allied mover, brought handtrucks, platforms, dollies, and the son of the owner to demonstrate and coordinate the heavy moving. Sixteen tons of boxes moved the 138 feet down the alley in less than two hours. The 370th Supply Company of the Army Reserve provided a full squad plus their training sergeant. Six college students, the army, a police sergeant (husband of a staff member), his husky sons, and I moved every box. All the little people and anyone who desired light work walked armloads of records and tapes around the perimeter of the block in human chains. The long route was established to allow the emptied record browser to arrive at the new building before the records. The moving equipment on wheels beat the kids every time. One little guy set the record with 122 trips. By 3:00 the library was taking shape in its temporary home.

Full library order was restored during the following week, when the remaining B. Dalton shelves arrived. A neighboring library closed for the day and sent the staff to Joliet to help. The 370th Supply and their two-and-a-half ton truck moved the shelves for us. Telephone lines for the multiplexer and computerized circulation and catalog system delayed the opening for an extra day as we waited for the Centrex computer to recognize the library lines from a new place. The annex opened for business on 6 June 1989.

Our computer run of overdue fire items was first produced on 20 June 1989. Since that day, the total of lost items has varied less than 1.7 percent, both up and down, as the nooks and crannies are truly inspected and contents of boxes and storage shelves are fully examined.

We immediately ran into thorny insurance problems, however.

a. The insurance policy was just ten days past a renewal for the year with changes in coverage. We had the binders, not the full policy. The adjuster (hired by the company) needed to see the policy to answer my questions about what it covered. In fact, he demanded the policy. The company took until the 14th of June to provide the policy. We disagreed with the wording in the policy defining coverage as "claims made." It should have read per-occurrence.

b. In 1989 we had spent months examining the adequacy of our coverage. Using the best risk management and loss prevention advice available, we had analyzed the structure and had designed coverage for our most probable levels of risk. We had determined that the structure would probably stand up well to a small fire. The structure did. The fire was contained in a relatively small area (25 percent of the first floor was actively involved). In short, JPL had just the fire we thought we planned insurance to cover. In subsequent emergency board meetings (before the fire), both the underwriter and the city's risk manager stated that they recommended higher coverage. Within the insurance community, the *actual cash value* of our valuable-papers coverage specifically covering books and the like is a completely subjective term. Initial statements about depreciation and the total value of the library collection, equipment, and so on from the adjuster indicated that we had a very tough battle for anything. *Replacement cost* is also fraught with pitfalls but appears to be a more rational coverage. The process works along these lines:

   i. Prove the title lost.
   ii. Order the title lost.
   iii. Upon receipt, send the bill to the company.

   iv. The value and worth of processing, freeze-drying, and so on are still subject to negotiation.

   v. You still must establish a value for the material that is not currently on the market, which is another negotiation. It does appear at this moment that one expert saying little value or one book dealer saying little value is acceptable to the adjuster, but one librarian or book dealer saying much value must be documented within an inch of its life.

   vi. On equipment, an accelerated depreciation schedule seems to be in use, much like a compact car. The day you drive it off the lot, it is worth half of what it just cost you. For every minute and mile, the value drops like a stone. Even replacement cost is debatable; in the area of salvage, the rule is to clean, and if that is not possible, then a desk is a desk is a desk (a shelf is a shelf, etc.).

vii. I listened to the adjuster's experts. I tallied up their comments on the building portion. The lowest numbers, regardless of their completeness, added up to their building-repair-portion offer. Eventually, the midrange estimates were recommended for our approval by our public adjuster and accepted by the company adjuster.

viii. A library collection, as a collection, has little or no intrinsic value in an insurance settlement. The very act of cataloging and keeping the item through the weeding and updating process should establish a professionally backed value of at least enough to update the inventory (including the catalog) and to seek a currently available substitute in the subject or type of material. Conversations with unknown persons at the "national library association," finally identified as the American Library Association by the company adjuster, resulted in very nebulous but low numbers for the value of juvenile nonfiction. Library literature does not record separate values for specific areas of the diverse collections of public libraries. An adjuster must protect the company and his or her standing with the company through a defensible settlement. He or she needs hard documentation for values, especially when the dollars add up to six or seven figures. I feel that the library profession must look to its state, regional, and national organizations for a value table that we can use across the country. The Joliet Public Library loss was centered in youth nonfiction, had $84,000 worth of new items not more than 4.5 years old, ane had the sources and titles that had stood the test of time and use against weeding since the founding of the library in 1875. The lost paperbacks and very popular sets have been replaced, in even greater numbers, through the donations of books and dollars by our customers. The insurance settlement should reestablish the 000-799 J core collection for our continued development into the depth and diversity the collection once had. Those statements are of no value to an insurance company about to put a number on a check.

ix. The library carried excess expense coverage only in the boiler policy. To reopen for business when one-half of the facility is out of commission for at least three months of work or at most nine months of work, the library must rent or rehabilitate space. Our excess expense (to run the business when the business place is out for a while) is draining the operating budget. The original agreement about space was a verbal okay to store books away from the recontamination area after they were cleaned. After the months of verifying and documenting there appears to be no dollars proposed to pay for the storage that was approved. The adjuster sent in a "quick estimate for set aside" to the company very early on, a reserve estimate. The claims manager then expected a similar number at the end of the process.

The hiring of a public adjuster (PA) was unnerving to the company man. It is claimed that action by us created an extra six months of lists and documentation. The company man was already demanding exactly that before we hired our expert. The PA did supply important manpower and expertise in examining the loss, preparing the claim, and establishing an expert opinion to protect the library board and staff from the 20/20 hindsight of "You should have done" or "You should have gotten more."

Practice

Are you and your organization ready for the next crisis? Have you formulated your plans? Are they current? Do your people know their responsibilities and authority during an emergency? Will your procedures work? These are just a few of the questions you must know the answers to if you and your organization are to successfully deal with your next crisis.

A crisis represents both dangers and opportunities. If your response to it is merely reactive, the dangers will outweigh the opportunities. The damage to you and your organization will be magnified by a public perception of failure, regardless of how good your response was. Even the most successful organization can be stigmatized unfairly for years to come.

On the other hand, effective crisis management can not only limit the actual damage sustained by your organization, it also permits you to affect the public's perception of the crisis. Effective crisis management can also pay dividends in terms of intraorganizational relations.

Increasingly, there are substantial financial, legal, personnel and other penalties attached to unpreparedness in the face of an emergency – especially when it can be established that a prudent person could have foreseen the possibility of the emergency. A crisis is not the time for ad hoc responses. Planning for all foreseeable contingencies is a form of insurance that should not be rejected. The relatively small commitment of time, personnel and resources is insignificant in the face of the possible damage from even the smallest disaster or induced catastrophe.[4]

In these introductory paragraphs of *The Handbook for Effective Emergency and Crisis Management*, Mayer Nudell and Norman Antokol spell out the challenges facing any agency when the inevitable disaster or induced catastrophe strikes. Gary Strong, the state librarian from California, is certainly another person to question about disaster preparedness. John DePew has outlined a statewide plan and has conducted workshops for Florida focusing on some of the techniques of preservation and recovery. Bridget Lamont, the director of the Illinois State Library, has disaster policies scheduled for all public libraries seeking per capita grants. Lisa Fox of SOLINET has outlined the regional and state perspectives in preservation.

The practice of planning is the best start. Using the crisis management pyramid from Nudell and Antokol's book, you see clearly why the Joliet Public Library is still recovering (see Figure 1).[5]

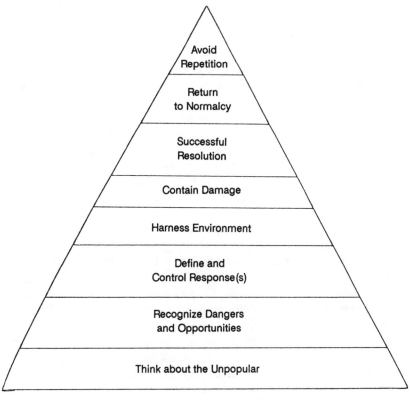

Figure 1. The Crisis Management Pyramid

I have covered many points that will confront every librarian faced with a disaster or a catastrophe. The base of the crisis management pyramid is to think the unthinkable. Until the top leader of an organization recognizes the importance of an issue, it rarely becomes more than another paper chase. If you are the leader, start the process. As the main character in Arthur C. Clarke's *2010* was given the unthinkable prospect, "Leave Jupiter orbit before the launch window for earth," you are given the challenge to examine your service for launching in a different direction. In the fictional case, the commander of the spacecraft, without damaging her credibility or judging the prospect, encouraged the crew to engage in the planning for an early launch as a "thought experiment." They were confronted with undeniable proof well after the beginnings of the "thought experiment." Had they wasted their time, they would have perished.[6]

You and your library have the time to engage in the thought experiment of disaster recovery planning. What you choose to do with that time is up to you. We used some of our time directly for disaster planning. When the event occurred, we had the outline of our plan to proceed while our grey matter was still reeling.

One starting point for planning is the examination of your policies and procedures. You can inventory the skills, knowledge, and expertise on your staff. Every workshop, every course, and every different background can be crucial to you at some point. Have you balanced the daily needs against the long-term risks recently?

You and your staff can begin the implementation of the disaster plan tomorrow. Practice focusing your perspective and recognizing the outside perception of your services and organization with your next press release, with your next meeting with the funding agency, or with your next public service exchange. I challenge each of you to examine your style and skills as a leader. Your individual practice time must be spent on becoming more effective.

"Good old fashioned Ben Franklin-style *character* is the key to building true, enduring success. Character alone gives you the consistent energy and know-how to pursue opportunity and the courage to prevail against challenges.

Beware of the superficial success formulas that focus on cosmetic skills and promise a quick fix. You simply cannot talk yourself out of problems you behave yourself into.

Character is a composite of one's habits. Because they are consistent, often unconscious patterns, habits constantly express our character and produce our effectiveness. Fortunately, for those of us not born effective (no one is), these habits can be learned.

"Habit 1: Be an initiator. Take charge of your life and actively shape it . . . learn to focus your efforts on things you can do something about."[7]

What happened! How many? How much? Who? When will the library reopen? All while you watch the fire fighters break out another window to ventilate the second floor and the investigators paw through the mashed and soaked books that should not be moved according to library conservation routines. Feelings of anger, hurt, and extreme insecurity will plague you. Thoughts of why, the swelling of the reaction to actively participate in the gruesome dismemberment of the heinous villain who has struck at your handiwork and livelihood, will occur even from the most gentle of staff members. Many staff members will clam up, some will store up the hurt and frustration, and many will surprise you in their adaptability and initiative. The positive theme was crucial. The establishment of a home for my homeless youth services department helped. An all-staff meeting for the release of the pressure, explanation of the facts, and establishment of a better rapport with each other was essential. The Inland Empires paper on coping with the Los Angeles Public Library fire was the core and basis for the presentation.

"**Habit 2: Begin with the end in mind.** If you are writing a mission statement," or a disaster recovery plan, "for your company, make sure that all employees are involved."

Three hundred thirty-nine of the 618 libraries in Illinois would have been wiped out losing the items Joliet lost. We are still in business. We have an opportunity to restart our youth services information base and update our collections.

"**Habit 3: Put first things first.** Set priorities and stick by them."

"**Habit 4: Think win/win, or mutual benefit.**"

"**Habit 5: Understand, then be understood.** Listen. Empathize. Understand."

The customer reaction was very intense. Many of Joliet's people felt as though they had been attacked. Our staff not only had to be treated for shock and fear, but quickly had to learn how to help our customers to cope with the shock, loss, and anger. We have had to cope with the uninformed gently, the impatient patiently, the paranoid sanely! All the while we have been defending the new addition, replanning all services and relocating them, establishing a tentative timetable for return, and reorganizing and preparing the new fiscal year budget (which, by the way, the city council adamantly refused to increase beyond last years' proposed level for various [political] reasons).

"**Habit 6: Create synergy.** Look for alternatives that benefit all parties and move beyond the original goals."

"**Habit 7: Sharpen the saw.** There are four dimensions to the human personality: physical, spiritual, mental, and social. Successful people renew themselves in all four areas daily."

Treat yourself as an important resource and make sure that proper rest, exercise and conservation of your spirit are placed high on the agenda. You cannot walk on water nor hurry the process through personal effort. You must lead and direct from a clear and rested mind. Treat yourself and your staff gently. Stay in touch often. Engage in humor and keep the fine points of human relations firmly in mind. It is too easy to snap and growl at people who are just as angry and hurt as you feel.

A good source of information is the *Illinois Basic Guidelines for Disaster Planning*. Also consider Dr. DePew's *Statewide Disaster Preparedness and Recovery Program for Florida Libraries*.

Nearly everything heard and seen in the Joliet fire emergency actions and in the followup are mentioned for your planning consideration. I cannot stress the importance of practice. In the wake of the fire, I had a chance to discuss the fire with the witness, that same computer operator who worried me so at first. His story goes like this: "I heard the sirens. I saw the flashing lights outside, so I went upstairs to see what was happening. I opened the door, saw the smoke, and ran back down the stairs and out the door. Which door? The one over by security, you know, the one we always use." Dull, right?

In reality, this story scared me more than the ambulance from the wrong fire station. My computer operator who has been with us for 7 years, through at least 10 emergency and security briefings and walkthroughs, opened a door from the fire stairs onto the first floor. He saw the smoke. He let the door close while he flew down the stairs right past the fire door we cut through the limestone and granite building for safety, down more stairs, under the fire, and he exited into the alley nearest the fire. In his haste, he was nearly run down by a responding firetruck. Why practice?

We have since rehearsed much more thoroughly for the real disaster possibility, people in the building. I can now guarantee that the Joliet Public Library staff knows where the nearest fire doors are. Do you?

You, the librarian or the staff member reading this report, will take these ideas to others in your library. What are you going to tell them? Exactly what will you start doing? I suggest that you start at once to think the unthinkable. Whatever the size of your library, you will be called upon to lead your staff through a frustrating and challenging time in the event of a disaster. You will be called upon to restore the normalcy to the emergency situation as soon as possible. You may be called upon to grab your emergency kit and head for a neighboring library. Are you ready?

If you have a choice, and you do not, never have a fire in the midst of renovating and adding to an historic building. To restore, renovate, and bring to full modern code compliance a 1903 stone structure – to add to it, repair it, and keep operating from it – adds real spice to the management and leadership life of its staff. Our customers, the readers in town, still occasionally ask, "What happened?" They say, "I thought that was all over!" or "I thought everything was burned up."

Without practice, how would you assess the damage? That is step one in the disaster recovery section of the Illinois guidelines. How replaceable is your collection? Exactly what will your insurance agent and company do in response to the call I so recently made? A written document about your expectations and their commitments can greatly ease the fears of all concerned.

Exactly what is covered, for how much, in what portion(s) of the insurance? Take out your insurance policy and read it. If there are any words you don't understand, get them clarified in writing. If there are processes described for co-insurance especially, have the company draft exactly how they will apply the various formulas listed in most policies to a hypothetical loss. Invite the loss prevention folks from the insurance company to inspect your facility. Incorporate their suggestions into your plans for funding and services.

Lobby your state library association to establish a study and recommendation committee to set a flexible set of values for library material. If the library associations can provide us with professionally supportable data, half the questions and demands for documentation for our insurance settlements can be made much less traumatic on the librarian coping with disaster. If a whole state association backs you, there is less challenge to the only expert on your library–you! Know exactly where you stand on values, and obtain professional support for that value. The more objective the source of the value, the less difficulty the insurance adjuster will have accepting it.

Examine your normal routines for having the emergency supplies on hand. Note our "routine" use of two water vacuums because our basement floods regularly or the use of trash bags and rolls of plastic, which the husband of one staff member purchased on his way down to see the library fire.

Investigate the inventory control system you use. How would you extract a listing of missing items with their values? Remember, our inventory lists work exactly backward to businesses that the adjuster who visits you will be used to. We check them out and expect them back. Only when they are overdue, do they become lists and values. If you do not have the item, how do you check it out? How do you separate the regular circulation from the special circumstances of disaster lists?

If your office was burned or closed to you for cleaning or deodorization, how would you run the library?

Have you made and stored in a fireproof file copies of programs and data for your library? I can tell you that the full contents of the business office could go! Do you have an updated bank set or an updated inventory stored remotely from the library?

Do you have emergency procedures and policies that work? Can you get your board or county authorities to spring for emergency procedures?

Which electrician knows your system?

Which plumber?

Who knows how to assemble and disassemble your shelving? In short, who could direct the removal of every shelf from an area without damaging it or losing parts?

Who knows the priorities of salvage, if there is time? Have you designated those priorities?

What buildings are available to use if you must reopen?

What other libraries or branches could "sub" for yours while you clean up?

Where do you rent things you do not own?

What do they have?

Can you locate chemically neutral cleaning items? Can you circulate or ventilate air?

Do your ducts have good emergency cutoff dampers?

Where does the electricity, gas, and water enter your building?

Do you have smoke or odor removal firms in your town?

If you had a broken set of windows, who would you call to board up the place or reglaze? Does the glazier have any glass of your size, thickness, and so on in stock? How long would it take for them to get your stuff? Would they stock some for use at the library? Would they be able to order any through normal channels?

Can you identify clay paper and ink types that will run? How about coated stock paper?

Until the fire, I thought I knew enough about the Joliet Public Library collection. I thought I knew enough about books and the like to be comfortable. The thought does not change the sinking feeling in the pit of my stomach as I made decisions on the fly that were far reaching in scope from skills and workshops too long passed to be clearly remembered.

Applied preservation and soot-covered conservation do not happen by accident. The need to be prepared for them does not. We don't plan floods, fires, tornadoes, hurricanes, burst pipes, and electrical fires; we react to them.

Already, the urgency of the recovery period has worn off in the eyes of others. At a recent review of letters of intent for LSCA funds, our research request for funding to provide a show and tell catalog of before and after appearances for juvenile material to be used if and when was rejected because "It's never going to happen again!" The study intended to provide a quick reference catalog with pictures and comparative costs for use when. That statement made me angry enough to burn. We must think the unthinkable and plan for the enormous task of doing what we must to restore our services from whatever happens. We must make the necessary decisions from the business, service, and public relations standpoints. The business decision of repurchase versus restoration is a very large one.

When the crisis, emergency, disaster, catastrophe, or tragedy occurs, the sum total of your preparation will be tested. Start now to become effective. If you have followed the recovery planning processes, the technical aspects of your next disaster are outlined. The most crucial factor in the recovery equation is you and your ability to seize the opportunities presented. Throughout library literature, the aspects of marketing the services are being stressed. Even if you have never marketed the library before, the immediate challenges and the perceptions of your responses to those challenges are your marketing of the library. If you fail to claim lost books on the insurance settlement because you could obtain a donated copy, if you make the business decision that these are replaceable for less than the salvage and restoration effort, you are the one who must both sell and live with that decision. The image of your professional perspective and the perception of your professionalism will stand up for you when your allies are disappearing. It may be lonely standing out front, but it is also rewarding. You are the leader first and the librarian second when disaster time rolls around. Prepare yourself and your staff for the challenge starting today. Whether the Joliet Public Library did the best job of recovery and restoration ever, or missed the boat, the comment from the Lions Club sums up the result:

"Jim, the last time you talked with us about the addition, we were worried that you lived in a world of books way beyond us. After seeing you on television during the fire, we wondered why we had not seen the full scope of the library before. Either you've gotten better, or we've learned something, but the Lions Club board voted unanimously to fund up to $6,000 immediately and up to $15,000 overall to implement that specialized service area when you move into the addition."

I have changed and grown with the challenges. I may be bored when all I have to do is run the library again, but the spirit of our library was born in fire!

What Can I Do Today?

1. Draft the disaster plan.

2. Engage in research to fill the knowledge gaps.

3. Work toward emergency ordinances.

4. Set up a line of credit.

5. Try to analyze insurance. (Eat a big deductible and get replacement costs are currently winning.)

6. Rebuild the collection (without the resources).

7. Lay the groundwork for the resources to fully rebuild service.

8. Repay some of the heartwarming professional dues with presentations such as this one.

9. Make up an at home packet of material for library board and staff of needed stuff.

10. Make the copies and store them as the computer database in a bank vault.

11. Rehearse and increase the responsibility load for many members of our staff who have proven their adaptability and worth under fire.

12. Set up the training mechanisms for crucial library skills that we sorely needed right then.

13. Begin the process of learning how to keep another public librarian or any other public official from the heartache, insecurity, and knowledge problems.

14. Explore with our professional associations a lobby for the support of our profession in crisis time: battles with insurance, auditors, public officials, and so on.

What Can I Do Tomorrow?

1. Examine the sufficiency of fireproof files for the storage of the important documents for the library.

2. Explore with the city fathers and the bankers how to establish an emergency line of credit without too much delay.

3. Set up the real priorities with your staff and post them for the fire department and the police department for salvage.

4. Examine alarms and detectors.

5. Examine the shelves and the materials.

6. Investigate water vacuums.

7. Make sure you have plastic to cover!!!

8. Ground and/or insulate the electrical box area.

9. Install smoke detectors (ventilation zones).

10. Investigate exhaust fans (how to dry things).

11. Identify what you want to preserve at all costs, and learn how to do it.

12. Rehearse the real tragedy–that is, people in the building when the disaster happens.

13. Revise the disaster plan. Rewrite it. Put it on the agenda for training, for review, for reading.

14. Knowing that 95 percent of the damage is water-based, decide what you would do about:
    a. Roof leaks.
    b. Burst pipes.
    c. Tornadoes, hurricanes, flash floods.
    d. Water mains, sewers.
    e. Covering or moving. (Where to?)
    f. Helpers who could be called upon.
    g. A portable phone or an agreement with the phone company about service, when and if.
    h. A list of your vendors and suppliers that is not in your office.
    i. Carpet cleaning, the person who does electrical work. (Arrange your credit with them.)
    j. Who does your shelving, who would sell you your next add-on.
    k. A portable computer that could support your office when the telephone service is back.
    l. Who on your staff know how your shelves come apart and go together.
    m. Fire exits (how you would get out, how would lead out).

The sum of the actions of the Joliet Public Library staff can be added up as follows:

1. Fire on 19 April 1989.

2. Donation center open on 24 April 1989.

3. Restoration Company hired on 28 April 1989.

4. Second floor (126,000 items in 8,400 square feet) cleaned, deodorized, and open for telephone information service on 5 May 1989 and for full service, including a fully wired and installed computer-served circulation desk on 6 May 1989.

5. Public Service Annex, Library Bounces Back Parade of Books, on 27 May 1989.

6. Old building cleaned by Friday, 26 May 1989

7. Donated bookstore shelves arrive on Sunday, 28 May 1989

8. Annex open for business on 6 June 1989. All boxes knocked down, all shelves in and arranged, MUX and phones in, circulation desk located and installed, full staff and public terminals available.

9. 24,000 donations screened. 14,000 added from May through September.

10. Grant spent.

11. Homework collection in place (one-half its former size) by 15 September.

12. And so on, until the collection is restored to its recommended "A" level in numbers and in depth.

Notes

1. Mayer Nudell and Norman Antokol, *The Handbook for Effective Emergency and Crisis Management* (Lexington, Mass.: Lexington Books, 1988), 3.

2. Kare Anderson, *Influence Institute Handout Material* (Illinois Library Association, February 1990).

3. Stephanie Matthews Simonton and Robert L. Shook, *The Healing Family* (New York: Bantam Books, 1984), 21-33.

4. Nudell and Antokol, 2-3.

5. Ibid., 21.

6. Arthur C. Clarke, *2010* (New York: Granada Publishers, 1982).

7. Stephen R. Covey, *Seven Habits of Highly Effective People* (Simon and Schuster: New York, 1989), as quoted in *Boardroom Reports* 19, no. 5 (March 1, 1990): 13-14. Each habit quoted in this essay is from Covey's work.

PART 2
Pressures on the Process of Scholarly Exchange

The Librarian's Response and Expectations

DUANE E. WEBSTER

Executive Director
Association of Research Libraries
Washington, D.C.

Research libraries and the process of scholarly exchange are under intense pressure. The need to communicate new knowledge, pressures on authors to publish, and publishers seeking increased profits and market shares have created a crisis for the academic community. (Figure 1 gives a summary of the information growth.) The problems are structural and chronic. The crisis must be addressed by the major partners in the information chain–the authors who create the valuable information; the institutions that support its creation; the publishers who deliver the finished products to the libraries; and the libraries that order, pay for, provide access to, and preserve the information. (Figure 2 shows just how many resources a library must manage.)

An important aspect of the current picture is soaring journal prices. The problem facing research institutions and their community of scholars is best revealed in a few summary statistics.

Figure 1. The Rapid Growth of Information

- One thousand books are published internationally every day.
- Nine thousand six hundred different periodicals are published annually in the U.S.
- More new information has been produced in the last 30 years than in the previous 5,000.
- The total of all printed knowledge doubles every eight years.
- The world's great libraries are doubling in size every 14 years, a rate of 14,000 percent each century.

Source: Richard Wurman, *Information Anxiety* (New York: Doubleday), 1989.

Figure 2. Current Information Resources Managed by Libraries

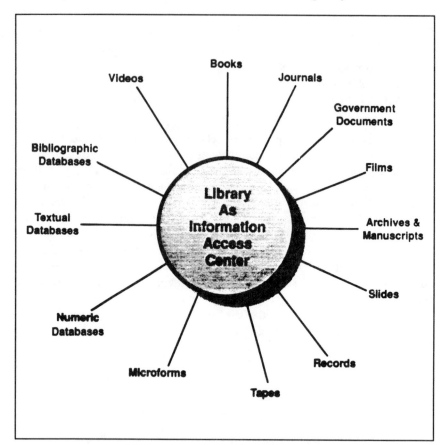

- During a recent 14-year period (1973-87), the average percent of all published serials titles held by research libraries dropped 4 percent (from 30 percent to 26 percent), despite an increase in funding support to libraries.

- During that period, the number of titles identified as being published worldwide grew from 70,000 to 108,590, an increase of 64 percent.

- From 1971 to 1988, the median purchase price of serials increased 350 percent while the mean overall expenditures of ARL university libraries grew by 234 percent. As university budgets have grown, libraries have slightly enhanced their funding in real income.

- From 1971 to 1988, the U.S. Consumer Price Index (CPI) grew by 182.5 percent. However, serials inflation of 350 percent has overwhelmed the increases in library funding. To hold serials acquisitions constant – let alone to add newly issued titles – would require a dramatic growth of library budgets.

- During the period from 1971 to 1988, the typical ARL library maintained materials expenditures at about 31 percent of total library expenditure. Mean expenditures for serials as a percentage of total expenditures on materials grew 16 percent so that by 1988 serials consumed 56 percent of the materials budget. At the same time the number of monographs purchased declined 15 percent.

- From 1975-76 to 1987-88, the average cost per serial in an ARL university library rose from 21.54 to 75.18, or 3 1/2 times its initial level. From 1986 to 1989 alone, we have been experiencing average increases in excess of 9 percent per year for U.S. serials and more than 18 percent per year for serials from foreign publishers.

- Although the average cost today of a U.S. serial is $85, this price masks the substantial variations in average price. Those changes have been documented for U.S. periodicals in 25 subject categories. The range of average price for U.S. periodicals by discipline is enormous. On the high end are chemistry/physics serials at $367; engineering, at $128; and psychology, at $114. On the low end are history, at $32; political science, at $45; and literature, at $29.

These data illustrate the impact high subscription prices have on all ARL libraries. It takes more money to build less comprehensive collections. I want to examine the serials issue as a symptom of the stresses and strains at work in the scholarly communication process. I will focus on recent projects related to serial prices: (1) the ARL serials initiative, (2) the recently established ARL Office of Scientific and Academic Publishing, (3) a study of serials prices being conducted by researchers at Utah State University,[1] to make available assessments of cost and value of serial literature.

The ARL Serials Initiative

I will start in reviewing the ARL serials project. Starting around 1984, serials prices increased rapidly, seemingly as a result of a number of factors including differential pricing, decline of the U.S. dollar in the international market, increased profit taking, and continued proliferation of publications. This phenomenon of increasing serials prices is now recognized as a cyclical process, with patterns of dramatic increases followed by library outrage that have occurred with regularity since the 1920s and prior to the 1980s, most recently in 1975-77. This time, ARL members find the acquisition pressure particularly troublesome because of the competing investments needed to automate library operations, introduce electronic information services, and address the preservation problem.

The ARL Committee on Collection Development began exploring alternative responses to the serials pricing problem by securing legal advice, investigating member responses to the crisis, and looking at other actions being taken to address the problem. It became apparent that the current crisis differs somewhat from earlier cycles because of the growing prominence of foreign commercial publishers, fluctuation of the dollar, and recent proliferation of titles and volumes of published research. The committee's discussions led to a proposal to secure objective outside analyses of price and cost patterns for targeted publishers, assess the causes of the current crisis, and develop responses to the crisis that might moderate price increases in the future.

The ARL reports break ground in significant ways. The first is in the use of outside specialists, Economic Consulting Services Inc. (ECS), to conduct a study. The research library community felt that a detailed study of price per unit (later defined as a page) over time (later set at 17 years) would give an impartial overview of what prices are doing. ECS also assigned costs to the serials publishing process and compared price increases over the years with publishers' cost increases over those same years. The objective of the economists' study was to test the hypothesis that *subscription prices paid by U.S. libraries have risen at a more rapid rate than inflation in publishing costs.* About 10 percent of the publishers' titles were selected at random for analysis. The four publishers targeted were Elsevier, Pergamon, Springer-Verlag, and Plenum. (See Figure 3.)

In its summary, the ECS analysis concludes that each targeted publisher has increased prices at a much faster rate than the rate at which publishing costs have increased. To make such determinations, ECS first created a scholarly publishing cost model, which they describe. The range of difference between the annual growth rates of price per page and publishing costs is from 2.6 to 6.7 percent. Over the period from 1973 to 1987, publishers' profit ratios are estimated at 40-137 percent.

Figure 3. Price-Cost Differential Growth Rates (1980-1987)

Publisher/Country	Percentage Growth in Price/Page	Percentage Growth in Costs	Differential
Elsevier/Netherlands	9.7	5.2	4.5
Pergamon/United Kingdom	15.4	2.5	12.9
Plenum/United States	11.4	3.4	8.0
Springer-Verlag/West Germany	8.5	3.4	5.1

Source: *Report of the ARL Serials Prices Project* (Washington, D.C. Association of Research Libraries), 1989, p. 23.

The economists suggested that, given these levels of profit ratios, the library community ought to stimulate greater competition among the publishers. Each journal is a unique product and competition does apply to the dissemination of copyrighted scholarly writings as it does to the production of aspirin or Christmas tree lights.

The second report, *Of Making Many Books, There Is No End*, by Ann Okerson,[2] makes its special contribution in describing the evolution of the serials crisis, assessing causal factors, and offering recommendations that would, to some extent, ameliorate the factors.

Figure 4. Causes of Serials Crisis

- Key role of commercial publishers.
- Exchange rate fluctuations.
- Publisher behavior.
- Growth in volume of research.
- Competition for promotion, tenure, and grants.
- Market dominance.
- Economics of journal publishing.

The causes of the serials crisis are described in detail. (See Figure 4.) There are a variety of factors to consider. First, the publication of certain key scientific and technical serials is increasingly concentrated in the hands of a small group of publishers. Elsevier (The Netherlands), Pergamon (U.K.), and Springer-Verlag (West Germany) together publish nearly 1,300 journals, many of the titles being leaders in their fields. The effect of this monopolization of library budgets was documented by Louisiana State University. Elsevier, Pergamon, and Springer together absorbed 43 percent of the increase in LSU's serials expenditures for 1987. Although their titles comprised only 2.5 percent of paid subscriptions, their cost consumed 20 percent of all serials funds.

A second major problem for American libraries in purchasing the products of international firms is the varying strength of the dollar. Research libraries spend as much as 60 percent of their materials budgets on non-U.S. materials. Particularly in the sciences, scholarship is increasingly international. A 1988 National Science Foundation study showed that between 1974 and 1984 references by U.S. scientists to articles by non-U.S authors increased almost tenfold and that articles with international coauthorship nearly tripled. Reliance on foreign subscriptions is a fact of life, and living with dollar fluctuations is a necessity.

A third factor is publisher behavior. Publishers justify their increases by claiming cost increases in editing, labor, and paper that have risen more substantially than the rate of inflation. Such growth in size carries a corresponding increase in price. Publishers also point to "twigging," which is when increased specialization causes an existing journal to split into several new titles. Publishers contend that photocopying and library resource sharing, which tend to decrease the total universe of subscriptions, have increased the cost per subscriber.

Publishers guard their pricing and profit structure jealously, and so the true differential between the prices and costs of publishers is unknown. However, a study by the Optical Society of America, which examined the cost in cents per 1,000 words for 40 optical journals, found that cost per 1,000 words varied from 2.6 cents to 94.7 cents, which translated into cost per page ranging from $0.3 to $1.05. As might be expected, more titles from commercial publishers appeared above the median than below it (14 titles above versus 5 below). In most instances, the cost of the commercial publications was found to be as much as more than 40 times that of the least expensive not-for-profit title. It becomes readily apparent that society journals are a better buy than commercial journals. As long as scholars favor commercial publishers over the scholarly society route for publication, however, libraries will have to acquire more expensive commercial journals.

Pressure to publish within the academic community is also a contributing factor. For example, the National Science Foundation reported that during the years 1982-88 the number of U.S. scientists and engineers doubled to over 4.6 million. These scientists and engineers publish more than a million articles every year in over 40,000 journals.

Competition for grants, government funding, and a secure tenured spot in the academic community places a premium on publishing. The National Science Foundation reported that 25 percent of practicing scientists work in academe but that 69 percent of all scientific publications came from academe. Just over one-quarter of the scientists are responsible for about three-quarters of the scientific papers.

The editorial policies of journal publishers also have a significant impact on the flow of serials literature. Symbiosis exists between editors and their publishers. Editors, who are often active scholars working in academe, are rewarded for producing bulk, and publishers profit because more and larger issues increase the profit margin. Success of a journal editor is frequently associated with the quantity of material published.

The Okerson study concludes with a number of recommendations. These include:

1. (This recommendation deals with effects.) ARL should undertake a set of urgent actions to demonstrate the serious and immediate impact of the serials crisis. ARL should appoint a staff officer to lead actively its efforts in the university, government, and publishing communities. Some of the possible actions enumerated are detailed price studies; research, education, and publicity directed at librarians, faculty, administrators, societies, and politicians; a clearinghouse role, coordination of protest actions; exploration of legal and legislative opportunities; better reviewing mechanisms; and correlation of price and use data to determine impact of readership of expensive serials.

2. (Recommendations 2 and 3 deal with causes rather than effects.) ARL should strongly advocate the transfer of publication of research results from serials produced by commercial publishers to existing noncommercial channels. ARL should specifically encourage the creation of innovative nonprofit alternatives to traditional commercial publishers.

3. ARL should strongly advocate that university administrations and granting agencies change their policies on judging promotion, tenure, and funding to minimize current pressures for excessive publication. (This recommendation calls to mind a Samuel Johnson quote, his reply to an inquiring author: "Sir, your manuscript is both good and original but the part that is good is not original and the

part that is original is not good.") While the academic community must avoid impeding the flow of genuinely new results, much of the publishing explosion appears attributable to the demands of authors, rather than of readers, and to the current method of judging academic success through publication.

The ARL Office of Scientific and Academic Publishing

At their 25 July 1989 meeting, the ARL board of directors agreed to establish a permanent addition to the ARL framework of capabilities. The addition, to be called the ARL Office of Scientific and Academic Publishing, would be directed toward understanding and influencing the forces affecting the production, dissemination, and use of scientific and scholarly information. (See Figure 5.)

Figure 5. ARL Office of Scientific and Academic Publishing Objectives

1. To increase understanding of publishing practices.
2. To encourage price moderation and quality control.
3. To promote consumer activism.
4. To strengthen roles of noncommercial publishers and government agencies.
5. To build collective responses with scholars and scientists.
6. To communicate with stakeholders.

Some of the objectives of this new office are:

- To develop a better understanding of the dynamics of scientific and scholarly publishing by conducting research and exchanging information on current practices and problems.

- To moderate the rate of increase of serial prices, provide information on prices and costs, publicize publishers' practices, and encourage the movement of publishing to nonprofit organizations.

- To provide consumer advocacy information to users and librarians and to address issues related to research library collection management and use. It is expected that the approved level of funding will allow a staged approach to building this new capability. At the outset, the office will focus on scientific, technical, and medical publications. Later, humanistic, historical, and social sciences publications will be included. The activities of the office will build on work going on in the profession and accomplished in the recent ARL serials prices project. The office, in the first few years, will serve as a clearinghouse for exchange of information and mobilization of action among interested parties. Initially, consumer advocacy and user education roles will be emphasized.

Some prospective projects and potential activities include:

- Working with scientific and scholarly societies to design and operate seminars on factors contributing to the information crisis.

- Promoting changes in the management of intellectual property rights, particularly in electronic formats.

- Reducing reliance on publication records as criteria for federal grants.

- Contributing to the development of the national network (NREN) as the vehicle for the exchange of research results.

- Encouraging experimentation in the area of electronic journals.

- Developing subject-specific cost indexes and price/use evaluation services for disciplines.

- Encouraging alternatives to commercial publishers, identifying problem publishers, and coordinating protest actions.

- Establishing buying groups of librarians and considering resource sharing.

This listing of possibilities is meant to illustrate the range of possibilities that will be evaluated once the office is established and staff recruited. This new capability addresses the need for more and better information by member libraries on the serials crisis. As a consumer advocate, ARL will provide research libraries, their users, and funders with better information with which to manage acquisitions and plan for the future. It is reasonable to anticipate that this office will attract media attention, encourage governmental attention, and exert ongoing pressure on publishers.

In the long run, the office will likely be evaluated in terms of whether librarians, with other members of the scholarly community, are able to influence future developments in scientific and scholarly communication. (Figure 6 lists some of the desired outcomes.)

Figure 6. Desired Outcomes of the Establishment of the ARL Office of Scientific and Academic Publishing

- Commercial publishers will moderate price increases.
- Not-for-profit publishers will strengthen their role.
- Library presence will be persistent, informed, and influential.
- Numerous experiments with nontraditional publishing will be tried.
- University practices in promotion, tenure, research, and publication will be changed.

The Utah State Study of Serial Prices

An interesting study is underway at the Utah State University. The key researchers are Kenneth Marks, Peter Wagner, Craig Peterson, and Steve Nielsen. They have sampled 466 titles over 20 years. The sample is larger than the ARL/ECS sample, and the time period covered is longer. They devised a cost model distinctly different from the ARL/ECS model, yet their findings complement the ARL/ECS findings and serve as a confirmation of the validity of the ARL/ECS study. The preliminary findings of the Utah State study state that from 1967 to 1987:

- In current dollars, *per page* cost went up eight times.

- In constant dollars, *per page* cost went up two times.

- Foreign commercial publishers are strikingly more expensive than domestic commercial publishers.

- U.S. noncommercial publishers are consistently the best buy.

Research libraries in the U.S. deserve a clear explanation of price increases that are well above inflation levels, especially those that are above industry averages.

Cost per Unit

Because of the escalation in the prices of scholarly materials these last five years both librarians and scholars have examined prices, particularly those of scientific journals, and speculated that certain titles, disciplines, or publishers may bear a disproportionate share of responsibility for price hikes. Such insights, if accurate, enable the purchasers to make more informed buying decisions and to ask appropriate questions of the producers. Publishers have countered this conclusion with the valid argument that a substantial part of the price increases has been the result of expansion in the number of published pages and articles, reflecting the growth of disciplines, and that looking at overall price increases does not accurately describe the pricing situation. In response to such very real concerns – perhaps in anticipation of them – members of the academic community have begun to do an entirely new type of pricing study.

These pricing studies analyze price per unit to estimate relative value. ARL has submitted a proposal to National Information Standards Organization (NISO) for a library materials price index that analyzes price per unit to create a standard methodology for studying the prices of printed library materials that will be useful and satisfactory to all members of the scholarly information chain – authors, publishers, and librarians.

This methodology will enable not only comparison of value for price within formats and disciplines but also comparison between formats and disciplines. For example, with such a standard it would be possible to compare value received from chemistry books as compared to chemistry journals, among specific publishers, between chemistry and mathematics, and so on. Scholars and librarians would have a clearer sense of what their money can buy. Publishers could compare their output more precisely with that of similar publishers. Such data potentially could make information producers more accountable for their pricing.

We also want to establish the basis of an international standard because publishing is increasingly an international matter and scholarship does not heed national boundaries. Also, we want to encourage more price-per-unit studies by a variety of participants.

Observations on Larger Issues

So far I have largely quoted and paraphrased from the ARL reports. Let me enumerate some aspects of scholarly publishing that this current crisis highlights.

What is the purpose of the scholarly journal? One objective is repeatedly stated: rapid publication of results. But journals, from the point of view of authorship, timeliness, and readership, are perceived very differently in different disciplines. In the humanities, for example, we are told that publication can be leisurely, even posthumous; for example, works by Heidigger and Wittgenstein appeared long after their deaths. Recent reading and conversations have reinforced for me the sinking feeling that because of the rapidity with which scientific tools improve and change, much published scientific research has a very brief half-life; in many cases, it goes unnoticed.

If many articles go unread, why not quit buying journals? New experiments with library online access to journal contents suggest that better access causes use to skyrocket. Perhaps one right answer is that libraries have not yet given good enough indexing to the insides of journals. Such evidence suggests that we need more rather than fewer subscriptions.

Along those lines, if press runs of scholarly monographs are as low as 300 copies and if the circulation of many scholarly journals is several hundred or less, is the scholarly publishing mechanism a dignified and socially desirable vanity press for researchers? After all, we know that close to 69 percent of published research comes out of academe. The author, however, does not pay the substantial charges of publishing his or her work. The library, and usually the taxpayer, are paying the price via acquisitions budgets. The publisher pays nothing to buy the work.

It has been suggested that librarians should promote electronic publications as the solution to journal problems, that perhaps the library community doesn't push the new technology hard enough. The evidence, however, is that librarians have been more assertive and coordinated about promoting new information technologies than any other members of the academic community and that the transfer process is moving along as rapidly as it can and perhaps more rapidly than the various protagonists can absorb or afford. Electronic acquisition is, as we have learned, very expensive. (Have you looked at a DIALOG rate sheet or a CD-ROM invoice lately?) It is also not *predictably* expensive. How does one anticipate needs in order to budget properly? Does one simply charge back, thus limiting information to those who can pay the high price? I believe that as costs are reduced, standards created, technical problems overcome, and user objections overcome, electronic dissemination *will overturn all ideas of what a journal is.* In the meantime, paper makes up the bulk of what libraries hold and work with, and it is what clients like.

Dialogue with publishers to achieve mutual understanding and solution has been a big theme for the past three years of so. I am becoming skeptical about what dialogue, at least dialogue with a number of the commercial publishers, can do. For example, I read that last year's profits for one major international umbrella publishing company was 25 percent, and, for another, 44 percent. This reminds me, again and again, that a dominant motive in commercial publishing is to produce a solid return on investment for shareholders. If that is the dominant aim of the commercial publisher, what true common ground has he or she with the education, public service, nonprofit sector? Some, but not enough common ground. Librarians partake in workshops with members of commercial publishers' staff, who are effective, conscientious, and caring about their jobs and customers. These are the people with whom the library community "dialogues." So the dialogue accomplishes but little. Perhaps it is with the wrong people. To use time effectively, the library community has to reconsider with whom to speak, who its natural affiliates are, and when dialogue becomes valueless. Perhaps it is high time to stop believing in the promises of riverboat gamblers.

I have some reservations about believing that competition will solve the price problem. A worst-case scenario is that competition will create yet more outlets for authors' output and will curse libraries with yet more demands on their already weary budget dollars. Instead of having one *brain research*, there could be several. That might aggravate rather then help the problem. When Eastern Airlines ran the only shuttle service between New York and Washington, the fare was $60. As soon as Pan Am competition was introduced, neither carrier was able to achieve as great a load factor, so fares went up. They are now $119 each way. The demand for scholarly articles is small and finite, far more finite than for the shuttle. Competition can be effective only if simultaneously the contributors have incentives to submit papers to the more cost-effective journals and to limit their submissions to real and nonduplicative results.

Conclusions

To be successful, the serials effort must be not only ambitious and collective but also coordinated and targeted. Until now, there has been a spontaneous outroar with no single organization assuming a coordinating role and with no agenda to focus activities. ARL, with its manageable membership size and common goals, its interest in scholarly publishing, and its commitment to the preservation of the body of knowledge, is a logical organization to undertake such a function. (Figure 7 lists the challenges confronting all research libraries.)

Figure 7. Challenges Confronting Research Libraries

1. How to manage the increases in scholarly publishing and find constructive responses to the serials crisis.
2. How to assess the ways information needs and use patterns will change over the next 10 to 20 years.
3. How to shape the production, marketing, and use of information in electronic formats.
4. How to integrate new information resources and services.
5. How to influence publisher behavior.

A lot of effort must be committed to informing the scholarly community at large. It is gratifying to see how much interest and concern the topics of serials quantity and prices generate and how many nonlibrary people wish to keep informed and involved in the next steps. Over the long run, it is only through an informed and concerned scholarly community that we can hope to address the structural factors causing the serials crisis.

I must conclude, then, that one of the reasons librarians have not been more successful in dealing with problems of serials prices and proliferation is that most of us simply have not paid persistent attention to the issues. If librarians are listened to, as they are, and if the community cares, as many do, it is time to adopt a new active stance within the academic community, no longer acting simply as middlemen or waterbearers of academe but as collaborators in the scholarly process. This active stance must be institutionalized.

I noted earlier that the problems facing the process of scholarly exchange are structural and chronic. They must be addressed by the major partners in the information chain. It is within the reach of all of us to influence future direction. Libraries can represent the best interests of their institutions by acting in concert and by facing commercial publishers with one cohesive voice.

The inability of our universities to buy the publications needed by their faculty and students is a problem that can no longer be ignored by either scholars or librarians. A satisfactory solution will require creative strategies based on a new partnership between librarians and scholars to advance their common interests. We must find ways to engage the problems and work together to overcome them.

Notes

1. Kenneth Marks, Peter Wagner, Craig Peterson, and Steve Nielsen, *A Longitudinal Study of Journal Prices in a Research Library* (Chicago, ed.; Association of College and Research Libraries, forthcoming).

2. Ann Okerson, *Of Making Many Books There Is No End: Report on Serial Prices for the Association of Research Libraries,* in Report of the ARL Serials Prices Project (Washington, D.C.: Association of Research Libraries, 1989).

The Publisher's Response and Expectations

BARBARA MEYERS

President
Meyers Consulting Services
Adelphi, Maryland

Once upon a time, publishers, librarians, and agents were all colleagues (friends even) and worked side by side to serve the larger scholarly community. Our jobs were to act as inconspicuous intermediaries in the transfer of ideas and knowledge from the scholar and researcher as author to the scholar and researcher as reader. We were expected to perform harmoniously under a cloak of invisibility–giving no interference to the higher purposes of our patron communities. Certainly we weren't expected to be intrusive by creating something as low on the scale of relevance as a *pricing crisis*. But, somehow, we have. We didn't do it alone, however; that, of course, is the rub and the cause of much consternation in and of itself.

Scholars at the moment are just barely becoming aware of the dilemma as libraries (aided and abetted by agents) confound and confuse them with practical questions such as: Which journals do you really need? Which journals can you do without? No, you can't have them all anymore. There just isn't enough money in the serials budget. Publishers have increased their prices too much for too many years. The university administration won't give us any more money for our acquisition budgets. So, you, the scholar, and we, the libraries, must suffer. Woe and alas!

Don't be dismayed, my scholar. We librarians and subscription agents are going to fight the publishers and force them to bring down their prices so that you may have all the journals you want, no matter what the quality, and the administration needn't give us any budget increases ever again!

Meanwhile, in the publishers' kingdom, envoy after envoy is sent to proclaim to the scholars that publishers do only what the scholarly research community asks. If the scholar wants tenure, then the scholar must publish enough to satisfy the university administration. The publisher exists only to serve that process. If the scholar wants a new journal, then the publisher is only too willing to oblige. After all, the scholar gives the publisher his or her raw material. We mustn't make the scholar angry. Just as in the kingdom of libraries, the scholar must be kept happy. That is becoming a more and more difficult task.

Wait! What is this I see on the horizon? Why it's publishers . . . and librarians . . . and agents . . . *and scholars . . . and administrators!* All have come together to solve the problem of equitable pricing for serials. It's just a matter of time before we will all be working as colleagues (friends even) again!

If only true life could be written to end as happily as a fairy tale. So simple. So straightforward. You always knew who was the hero and who was the villain. Now it's not such an easy matter. Upon honest examination of our situation, I believe that everyone involved in the scholarly communication process would admit that each of the players – scholars, publishers, librarians, administrators, and agents – has contributed to the pricing dilemma that is food for so much recent debate.

The great current debate between two of the major players in the process – publishers and librarians – was stirred considerably by the release of the *Report of the ARL Serials Prices Project* in May of 1989. Did the report aid in our search for a solution? Or did it merely "muddy the waters"?

I was fortunate enough to have been taught the skills relating to technology assessment by Dr. Joe Coates, who was at that time associate director of OTA, and he counseled us that one should start off with three good comments before ripping a work apart when carrying out a solid, critical review. In an attempt to prove that I learned my lessons well, let me make a few positive comments about the *ARL Report*.

First, it is important to the library community. The funding and fulfillment of the contract were a united front that displayed a deep concern on the part of the library community as a whole over the pricing issue. The extent of financial backing and ultimate endorsement for the study was a rare show of cohesive thinking from librarians, even if officially only from those belonging to the ARL.

Second, given the nature and limits of its resources, ECS performed admirably. I had the president of one of its major Washington competitors review the report. His assessment was that, given the fact that even within the body of the work ECS cites every instance where numbers are suspect, he had never seen a more honest report from any economics consulting firm.

Third, the report has been a valuable tool in heightening the awareness of many publishers of the attitudes and opinions of the library community. I certainly urged all my clients along with all my publishing colleagues to read the report from cover to cover. I hope that the results of that encouragement can be proved by the number of copies sold!

Now then, line-by-line nitpicking aside, I do find fault with the report in the following major areas.

First, I have to challenge the basic premise that any industry can go in and examine another's internal minutiae and do it well!

Second, as a researcher myself, I can only presume that the studies were either underfunded or poorly constructed in terms of the methodology with regard to data collection in both the ECS and the Okerson efforts.

Third, the study contributes to a potential chasm within the publishing community, especially between large commercial houses and the professional society publishers, that might ultimately harm the very fabric of how we, as publishers, do business, especially with regard to how we interact with our major customer base, the library community.

A point of truth, my third comment is not isolated to the ARL report alone. It has become more and more a matter of fact, not speculation, that the publishing community is divided along the lines of profit versus not for profit as well as between STM (scientific, technical, and medical) versus the arts and humanities. Just as we see the potential for the development of a "have and a have-not" society concerning information *access*, so too I see similar developments occurring with regard to which information *producers* (i.e., publishers) will survive into the next century.

Duane Webster in "The Librarian's Response and Explanation," has commented that journals are concentrated in the hands of commercial publishers. Perhaps this is true when you count *titles*, but it is not necessarily true when you count *pages* – the sheer bulk of information produced. In the most recent of the price studies I have conducted for the Optical Society of America, it was found that professional society publishers produced, on average per journal, *nearly four times as many pages* as their commercial counterparts!

I am glad to see that Duane does not tar all publishers with the same brush. Good scholarly publishers are out there, and they are the majority of the publishing community. However, almost all publishers have a problem with Ann Okerson's recommendation that there should be a shift of scholarly publishing to "noncommercial channels." Okerson is advocating that this shifting be prompted through the funding agency mechanism. Publishers view this as a potential infringement on an author's first amendment rights to publish wherever the author deems it most appropriate; tying the financial resources for research to where the researcher may ultimately publish the findings is a very dangerous suggestion.

Bette Davis once said: "I prefer it the hard way. If it's too easy, what is the accomplishment?" I submit to you that if we also "prefer it the hard way," then this current situation is a fairy tale come true. There is much to be accomplished in the area of serials pricing, and to do so we must move forward with some creative problem solving. I recommend to all the players involved in our situation a small book entitled *Getting to Yes: Negotiating Agreement without Giving In*. The authors, Roger Fisher and William Ury, state their premise quite succinctly in the introduction about the three ways to negotiate: soft, hard, and *principled negotiation*. Developed at the Harvard Negotiation Project, principled negotiation is the method based on deciding "issues on their merits rather than through a haggling process focused on what each side says it will and won't do. It suggests that you look for mutual gains wherever possible, and that where your interests conflict, you should insist that the result be based on some fair standards independent of the will of either side. [It] shows you how to obtain what you are entitled to and still be decent."[1]

Above all else, I sincerely believe that most publishers, most librarians, and other involved parties who are truly concerned with the future well-being of the scholarly communication process wish to be decent in their negotiations.

As a Sister Sledge song says, "We Are Family." But what kind of a family are we? Cleveland Armory, in *Who Killed Society?* wrote, "A good family is one that used to be better." I ask librarians, agents, and any scholar or dean who may be reading this, Will you join me in attempting to make our family better again?

Librarians and publishers are the married partners in the family, and, as in any marriage, there is sometimes trouble in two areas: sex and money. Being in polite company, let's not talk about sex, and let's agree that (for some) the money is getting better. But, the little bit of money that's coming in may just be masking some deeper problems that are still there.

We must realize that we now exist in a balloon environment. If we exert pressure at one point, the problem will shift or be made worse in another part. We must all be conscious of our actions and of how they affect another "family" member. Publishers are concerned right now with maintaining current revenue levels for journals whose circulations in the institutional marketplace are eroding anywhere from 3 percent to 6 percent (and higher for some titles) each renewal cycle. Every canceled subscription now contributes to a higher subscription price next year. Until publishers can break that spiraling cycle – one hopes with the assistance of scholars, librarians, and university administrators – not much change can be expected in the current scenario.

We can only be part of the solution if we recognize and admit that each and everyone of us is part of the problem. We must accept our share of the blame and work on our part of the process with concern and input from our sister or brother next to us. As Christopher Morley once said: "Only the sinner has the right to preach."

I am in complete agreement with someone most librarians know very well, Deana Astle of Clemson University, when she writes in the *Journal of Academic Librarianship*, "Severe pressures such as static library budgets, rapidly increasing prices, and escalating article production are forcing changes in the scholarly journal. It will not soon disappear, however, since no acceptable alternative is yet available. Authors, librarians, publishers, and university administrators need to address the underlying problems of the scientific information chain, for which skyrocketing prices and burgeoning journals are but symptoms, if the scientific communication system is to continue to function."[2]

In fact, one of the underlying problems of "the scientific information chain" is the sheer number of researchers now publishing in our journals. At the Society for Scholarly Publishing "Future of Scholarly Journals Seminar" held in Chapel Hill, N.C., I submitted, and I do so here as well, that the ever-growing number of articles that is firmly based on the increase in researchers since the last World War is, in fact, "the price we pay for peace." We can live peacefully with all those authors if their universities will extend tenure on the basis of the *quality*, rather than the *quantity*, of publication.

This one area is the first where we can all become more cooperative in the future, that being *quality control* of publication. We must start at the beginning with authors, and address each and every virus and bacteria that has invaded our system – from authors forced to "publish or perish" to publishers forced to sustain many journals on the revenues of a few to librarians receiving insufficient funds for acquisition and preservation to universities being less than the number-one priority in our nation's attempt to maintain its international position.

A recent attempt to make scholars and authors more aware of the situation was made at the American Association for the Advancement of Science (AAAS) Annual Meeting. Dr. Fred Spilhaus, executive director of the American Geophysical Union; October Ivins, head of serials at Louisiana State University; and Karen Hunter, vice-president of Elsevier Science Publishing Company presented their viewpoints.

I was especially proud of Fred Spilhaus when it was reported in the *Chronicle of Higher Education* that he "urged scientists to avoid buying or submitting papers to high-priced journals that are of low quality." Likewise, I was pleased to learn that October Ivins placed some options for remedy before the assembly by suggesting that more journals be published by the more cost-effective professional society publishers and that there might be "revisions in the system of awarding grants and promotions that emphasize the quality of professors' publications rather than their quantity."

I was dismayed, however, at the tone supposedly expressed by Karen Hunter, one colleague and friend whom I had long held as one of the most thoughtful and insightful professionals in publishing. The *Chronicle's* reporting leads one to believe that the bulk of her presentation was a rallying cry against her sister publishers, the not-for-profit professional societies. Thus, some of my earlier comments about rifts within the publishing community are already being substantiated. I must admit that in the recent OSA price study, which I quoted earlier, the results were so one sided that the only reasonable title for the article was "Research Shows Societies Publish, Price Journals Competitively."[3]

However, Karen did cite one important factor that was reported. It is at the very heart of the current situation: "It is not journals which create articles, it is the research community that creates articles. The journals reflect that community. When the scientific communication and reward structure de-emphasizes publication, journals will decrease accordingly, and probably not before."

As I have said in several library meetings, good publishers want librarians to work with their faculty and their technical staff to exercise increasingly demanding purchase behavior. We believe heartily in the concept of collection development versus comprehensive collecting. We applaud librarians who practice cost-benefit analysis in their decision making concerning journal and book acquisitions.

Lisa Fox has coined a maxim, "Acknowledge that cooperation is an unnatural act." I almost feel as if I'm asking us all to commit some kind of perversion by wanting my family back together – and cooperating – again. I want to get to that elevated state in Jim Johnston's crisis management pyramid. That is, we need to return to normalcy and, more important to avoid repetition of our current state.

Notes

1. Roger Fisher and William Vry, *Getting to Yes: Negotiating Agreement Without Giving In* (New York: Penquin Books, 1983).

2. Deana Astle, "The Scholarly Journal," *Journal of Academic Librarianship* 15, no. 3 (July 1989): 151.

3. *Optics & Photonics News* 1, no. 2: 21-24.

PART 3
The Role and Effectiveness of the Public Library

Conflicting Roles of the Public Library

CHARLES ROBINSON

Director
Baltimore County Public Library
Towson, Maryland

Nineteen-ninety is bad enough – what really terrifies me is that the year 2000 is only ten years away! We're dealing in this conference with "Issues for the New Decade." In the later years of the decade, I'm sure we'll all be attending conferences promising to identify the "Issues of the Next Century." Having been around for so long, I am familiar with this propensity to forecast by decades. We did it in the fifties and looked forward to larger chunks of time such as the "last half of the century" – the twentieth century, not the twenty-first!

Preservation, the serials dilemma, and the public library are issues all right. Whether or not they are issues for the new decade, even in librarianship, is another issue in itself. As a public library director, I consider both preservation and the serials dilemma to be minor issues. I might even go so far as to say they are *nonissues* to me. In a recent issue of the *Baltimore Sun* was a review of the futurists' forecast for the 1980s. The scorecard showed that "of all the missed forecasts in the decade, technology was the worst." So, whether or not the issues discussed here are really issues for the 1990s is obviously yet to be decided.

Conflicting roles for the public library – is this an issue for the new decade? Or, for that matter, an issue for the new century coming up? Sure.

You bet. Of course, to be really truthful, it was an issue for the *1890s*, too, and certainly an issue for the *last* new century, the twentieth century!

"We learn from experience that men never learn anything from experience" (George Bernard Shaw). It's pretty evident from reading the history of development of public libraries in this country that a single prominent role was seen as the responsibility of public libraries – self-education. Another, less-defined role was given to libraries, that of "arsenals of a democratic culture," whatever that meant. Of course, what constituted "education" and "culture" was pretty much left up to the definitions made by librarians, who, in the words of Wayne Weigand, a library school professor who has written about this period, saw themselves as the "apostles of culture."

In any event, self-education, however fuzzily defined or by whom, was the general role seen fro public libraries. Nobody thought much more about it, apparently, and librarians occupied themselves with doing things like inventing classification systems, putting books on or taking books off the open shelf, arguing about buildings – in other words, pretty much as we do now – anything to avoid thinking about really difficult questions with no easy answers, questions concerning mission or roles, for example.

Over the years, however, the picture was changing. America was turning its immigrants into Americans; public education was gaining not only in effectiveness but in extensiveness; books were getting cheaper in relation to personal income; and leisure time was more and more available. Along in here somewhere, public libraries added two things that did more to change their roles than anything else until the '80s: fiction and children's books. Don't ignore here the concomitant rise in competition – school libraries, book clubs, and bookstores – which themselves carried more and more fiction and children's books.

Without noticing it, as it were, public libraries were adding to their role the most insidious factor of all: reading for entertainment, or "leisure reading," or "trash," depending upon your outlook. But we were still defining our role generally as self-education. Remember the "people's university"?

We never gave up one thing as librarians, however. We still saw ourselves as apostles of culture, as "arbiters of values, as definers of access, as keepers of order, as true intellectuals, and as controllers of supply and interpreters of demand," (to quote myself in a recent *Library Journal* article). Most of us still defined our role quite simply as that of supplying the materials and organization of knowledge to assist the self-educator. Frankly, I think we still do, with the addition of semiteaching roles as readers' advisors, information specialists, children's specialists, and so on, none of these, of course, inhabited libraries in the first quarter of this century. All it really took in the matter of qualification to work in a public library was a sufficient measure of gentility, overlaid with a frosting of culture – the kind of culture depended on where the library was. Culture in the early years of this century was less affected by the presence of the screen or the tube. "Culture is an instrument wielded by professors to manufacture professors, who when their turn comes, will manufacture professors" (Simone Weil).

This whole business of self-education, the continuing growth of libraries, the acceptance of tax support for public libraries, the increasing specialization, and, perhaps most of all, the "professionalization" of librarians led to the most crippling curse ever laid upon the public library mission in its history, the central library in a city. A number of factors, in my view, helped to bring upon the unsuspecting users of public libraries the growth of this burden. This burden has in all major cities in the United States and in many smaller ones (but not yet in most suburbs) led to the death throes of the public's library, the community library

How did I ever get this crackpot idea? It was put in my head about 20 years ago by F. William Summers, a name you might recognize. When he was at an institution whose name I have conveniently forgotten, he (or one of his minions) half-completed some research that generally indicated that the more of your available resources you put into the central library, shortchanging the branches, the less use you get of the system as a whole, including the central library. I don't believe this led the eminent Dr. Summers to the same conclusions, or at least the same *expression* of those conclusions, as I reached. He certainly has, however, gone on to great honors in the profession, to say nothing of appointments to prestigious positions. I, on the other hand, have been recently described by one headhunter as "not an acceptable candidate for any major job placement from our company." So much for attacking the conventional wisdom in a confrontational manner.

Where Are We Now?

Where are we *now*, as a profession, in our perception of roles of the public library? Why are we even here considering roles at all? The business of roles, of mission, of planning for public libraries, has all come about in the past 20 years because on occasion members of this profession, particularly in our professional association, ALA, consider and question the conventional wisdom.

In the 1930s, 1940s, and 1950s, the theoretical method of telling whether a public library was "good" or not was whether or to what degree it met standards – that were set by professional associations, not necessarily by the community. That's not all bad, obviously, or at least the process is good enough for the academic libraries, hospitals, schools, and so on. People are still trying to do it for public libraries, although the Public Library Association, the standard setters of ALA for public libraries, has abandoned the process of quantitative standards as unworkable, unjustified, and inappropriate.

"I'm an idealist: I don't know where I'm going, but I'm on my way" (Carl Sandburg). The trend in the Public Library Association in the past 15 years has been increasingly pragmatic about the diversity of the library's public and the differing resources and demands of communities across the nation; nationwide standards, expressed in anything other than idealistic terms, did not begin to address these differences.

In 1984 Nancy Bolt, now state librarian in Colorado and then president of the Public Library Association, appointed a committee that she optimistically named the New Standards Task Force, indicating even then the yearning to return to the old quantitative standards used so widely and so ineffectively for years to beat on the heads of generally unresponsive appropriating authorities.

This committee started off rejecting the whole idea of standards, in the first 15 minutes if I remember correctly, and they were never mentioned again. Planning, performance measures, mission, and roles were; you can see the magnificent results in the ALA publication of 1987, *Planning and Role Setting for Public Libraries*.

PLA's New Standards Task Force was a successor to other committees that had been tackling the difficult matter of standards. PLA's Goals, Guidelines and Standards Committee, for example, had recently produced the widely used first edition of *Output Measures for Public Libraries*. Made up of twelve members representing fairly, I think, the spectrum of different sizes of libraries, including state library agencies, the task force met for hours and hours, over years and years, working out the Public Library Development Program. This program was made up of three publications, one on planning and role setting, one on output measures (the second edition of the original classic authored by Joey Rodger and Doug Zweizig), and a serial publication issued annually called the *Public Library Data Service*.

There were incessant arguments and shouting matches, but unlike many other ALA committees, no cabals, private agenda, or personal vendettas. It was, for us all, a continuing high level of professional stimulation, with always, at least from my perspective as a member of the committee, an underlying appreciation of the public library users' viewpoint and ownership stake in the institution we were so endlessly dissecting and analyzing.

While every member of the task force contributed both pragmatically and ideologically to the discussions, what I remember most vividly were the clarity and problem-solving expertise of Ron Dubberly, now the director of the Atlanta-Fulton Public Library. Ron writes what I can only describe as turgid prose. When he speaks, he generally mumbles in some strange Floridian dialect. Upon careful and conservative reflection, however, I would suggest that almost everything innovative and certainly a great deal of the change occurring in public library philosophy and management is traceable to some idea, thought, or action by Ron Dubberly. Working behind the scenes generally, although he has served as president of the Public Library Association, his contributions to the profession, at least in the area of public library philosophy, can be traced back about 15 years. His kind of quiet, persuasive, but nevertheless pervasive influence seldom receives the credit it deserves.

Ron Dubberly is, of course, a graduate of Florida State University. I'm sure that all library schools have their distinguished graduates, but as far as I am concerned, speaking as a public library director, Ron has done more for public libraries than any other library school graduate in this generation. If honorary degrees were given for really significant accomplishments rather than for financial contributions or commencement speeches, Ron should have collected some by now.

Ron's has come up with absolutely great ideas. Much of the conversation about public library roles was put into perspective by him. There are, as you know, eight roles. Since the publication of the eight roles, my library, along with hundreds of others, has gone through the process of role identification and selection. The process is interesting, but even more important is the continuing thinking about roles I have to go through, practically on a daily basis, when assigning priorities for limited resources. In words that are more understandable to me and to my staff–do we put our money where our mouth is? I'm not always sure, and I think it's because I'm constantly in the process of finding out what our role really is, rather than what I or my board or the politicians or the profession or the user himself or herself *thinks* it is or *wishes* it were.

First of all, let's look at the really big library roles. Most libraries supported by tax funds are school libraries, academic libraries, or public libraries. Most people, including librarians, think of themselves as libraries–just libraries, with little thought about the tremendous differences in mission–that make them, in my view, completely different kinds of institutions with different requirements in almost all aspects of operation, whether it be staff qualification, materials selection, buildings, equipment, philosophy, or operation. Library schools and librarians say, "Well, they all have people and books, and isn't that the essence, the core of librarianship?" Nonsense. The people all have different outlooks, the books are largely different titles, the buildings and equipment should be different even if they aren't, and the philosophies and measures of effectiveness are totally different. They are as far apart as communism and capitalism, both economic systems, or as battleships and sailing ships, both ships, or perhaps, as male and female, both the same species. One is not better than another. They have, however, differing function or, as I should say here, differing roles.

Libraries, in the hearts and minds of ordinary people, all fall into the same mold, or seem to. This is understandable for ordinary people, who spend very little of their time in libraries. What is harder to accept is that librarians and library associations like ALA do pretty much the same thing. I might pretend that I am interested in the serials dilemma. My library doesn't *have* a serials dilemma – and if it did, it shouldn't. And except for a few local history materials, which I think about for seven minutes on the fourth day of months that have an *R* in their names, preservation of materials doesn't enter my mind. Other librarians think I should be ashamed of this attitude, but really I'm not. I find very few librarians in schools and academic libraries worrying about the property tax, diesel engines on bookmobiles, the shelf life of videos, or children's day care – all of which take a great deal of my time and attention. These issues are even more important than the federal legislative agenda, which, I say (very, very quietly) is not very important to day-to-day public library operations, at least in its present form.

The Roles of Public Libraries

Public libraries serve children and students, but they are not school libraries and we are not teachers. We serve adults who seek education, self-education, but we are not academic libraries. You have to be able to read to use books, which is one of the formats we have in public libraries, but we don't know the first thing about the teaching of reading and have no responsibility for the level of illiteracy in this country. We have reference materials but little, if any, material for original research. We are not homes for the homeless; we are not the guardians of the western literary tradition; we are not the financial support of little-known poets; we are not, in the words of Marvin Scilkin, "kennels for the publishers' dogs." We are not a lot of other things that well-meaning librarians who are closet social workers, teachers, literature professors, architects, or decorators would have us be.

But of course we are these things. We have to be all of these things because those who support us expect us to be, at least to some extent, just as they expect schools to be babysitters, parents, ministers, coaches, restaurants, as well as teachers.

All public libraries are tax supported, and at the local level, we are, in the deathless words of my county executive, "closest to the people." As such, we must meet the public's expectations. This does not, to a good manager, mean always supplying those materials and services that people *say* they want, but it does mean that you should supply the materials and services the people – and here I must emphasize that I mean *most* of the people, not *all* of the people or a small segment of the people – actually use. That's why marketing is important. We, as librarians, too often supply to our users what we feel they should read, the services they should use, without any real attempt to find out what they in practice *do* use or borrow, regardless of what they *say* they read or borrow.

Whatever public libraries are, however, they are *not* academic libraries, although we seem to have enough public librarians who are closet academics to staff several large university libraries. They are mostly, of course, housed in the larger cities. By being in the central libraries, where the administrators are housed, and in many cases being the administrators themselves, they have turned many of the nation's public libraries into quasi or semiacademic libraries, apparently hoping to serve a constituency that not only doesn't exist, but never has existed to any significant degree in the public library domain.

When people, even librarians with masters' degrees theoretically skilled in the reference interview, hear this, they assume I have some quarrel with academic librarians. Far from it–they are absolutely necessary to staff academic libraries, which have a great importance to the institutions they serve and to the students and researchers who use these institutions. So let it be clearly said here, no matter what you personally may feel for or against academic libraries or librarians, my purpose here is not to criticize them in any way. They seem to be quite good at doing that to each other. If they try to infiltrate public libraries and turn them into these quasiacademic libraries the public doesn't need and doesn't use, however, that's a different story.

Unfortunately too many librarians either won't or can't understand the role and mission of public libraries. First, they don't appreciate or understand that public libraries are paid for by *all* the people–people who want preschool reading in great quantities for their children, people who want the public libraries to have collateral and supporting materials for their elementary and secondary education that school libraries don't have either the money or the space for in this age of increasing emphasis by the schools on homework. The taxpayers also want copious amounts of nonfiction–not the titles generally represented in academic libraries, but cookbooks, travel books, auto repair books, and books about politics, religion, cosmetics, and practically any interest you can name. They want any fiction, including what some libraries call trash and some call classics. Don't forget, Dickens was the "trash" of his day, as was Scott and maybe even Shakespeare.

I'm really, really sick of librarians. Librarians who do not work in community or town libraries, but rather in central libraries or the local college library, put down by implication the people who pay for materials and services of the public library. One recent example of this was an article by a "librarian who has worked in the New York and Brooklyn public libraries" in the 16 February 1990 issue of the *New Republic* (reprinted in the February 17 issue of the *Baltimore Sun*). He described what he perceived as the loss of balance between the functions of the public library to provide leisure reading and to be an educational resource. He said that "trash fiction, celebrity biographies and diet-fad books increasingly constitute the core collections of many of our public libraries." He goes on to cite the core of public libraries' traditional constituency as the "serious adult reader."[1] What utter sanctimonious twaddle. Who appointed this man to characterize anything as trash? Is a biography of Eisenhower or Bush a celebrity biography? What diets are fads and what aren't? Does he know?

The business of attaching *your* values to the practice of materials selection, rather than responding to the legitimate demand of the public, is all too prevalent in collection development. (Actually, *collection development* should be a term banned in public library management. We have no business "collecting" anything. That implies you don't ever get rid of anything. I feel strongly that the real test of the quality of a public library is not what you buy, it's what you discard as no longer useful. Let's call the process *stock development*, or *inventory control*, which of course are both terms repugnant to the elitist.)

There is, out there, a large flock of librarians who very, very badly underestimate the intelligence of the American public library user, and the New York librarian who wrote that article is one of them. Because they are not interested, perhaps, in Orwell or Nietzsche, they are not "serious readers." Balderdash. I certainly consider myself a serious reader, but I read chiefly in the field of British naval history and wouldn't touch Orwell or Nietzsche with a ten-foot pole. I certainly qualify as a reader of trash in his mind, I guess, because I've read everything Tom Clancy and Alexander Kent ever wrote. My daughter, who has her master's degree in library science from Simmons, can't wait for the newest Danielle Steel. Let me tell you a couple of secrets: There are a lot more taxpayers out there who read Danielle Steel than who read George Orwell, and there are more who would rather read Peale than Nietzsche. Don't tell me that they can buy their books in paperback at the local supermarket. Sure they can, but for a person who reads only three books a week, say, that's $15 a week after taxes. Why should they do that when they pay their taxes? Should they do so to allow that 1.2 percent of the public who reads Orwell and Nietzsche to find a copy on the shelf of their local branch? How unfair!

So the basic role conflict we have here is a conflict in perceptions, perhaps, based on all sorts of assumptions carelessly made. The librarian who attacked the selection and display of materials in Brooklyn, Queens, and Baltimore County libraries almost certainly has no knowledge, because he hasn't bothered to find out how many titles each library buys annually, how many copies of these titles they buy, and how the public actually uses the books that are bought. One of the most peculiar assertions made by people like these is that a public library should have a copy or copies of a particular title whether anyone reads it or not on the hope, I suppose, that maybe someone will, sometime, some year or another (if it hasn't crumbled into a yellow dust). The title, incidentally, that is usually given as an example is something almost always from English literature—perhaps American—that the critic has read and loved. Seldom does the critic mention economics, cookbooks, or even history. I have never been able to figure out why a public library would keep a title no one has borrowed for, say, two years. I would guess that a statistical study would show that, if a book had not circulated for two years, the chance that it would in the next dozen would be about 10 percent, if that. I'd further venture the guess that, even if you set the circulation standard of once every *four* years and discard everything that doesn't meet that very modest criterion, you'd eliminate 50 percent of the collections of every public library building housing 500,000 books or more. Of course, at the same time you'd save millions and millions of dollars in staff time, heating and cooling costs, capital expenditure for expansion, and so on.

The role describing a public library as a sort of savings bank for books no longer read is an inappropriate role for a public library, even if perfectly appropriate for some academic libraries, and further confuses both librarians, who should know better if they intend to fulfill any purpose other than custodial, and the public, which expects resources to be spent to benefit its present-day needs.

When public librarians, trustees, and the public itself really understand and appreciate the differences in roles between the public library and the academic library—an understanding that is obviously a long way from being anywhere near universal—about three-quarters of the battle to assure adequate public libraries to meet the needs of the public will be won.

The remainder of the difficulties and challenges lie within the eight roles for public libraries cited in *Planning and Role Setting*, along with the basic management that would assign resources in accordance with the roles chosen.

If you look in another annual publication of the Public Library Association, the latest of which is *Statistical Report '89*, you will find all sorts of interesting statistics about public libraries, that tell much about what our priorities are and whether or not the priorities we list are real or not, based on the story told by other statistics.

First of all, according to the PLA manual, only two out of eighteen public libraries serving one million or more people report that they have selected roles at all. These libraries are the Free Library of Philadelphia and the Miami-Dade Public Library System. No one else.

This is surprising because my observation is that large libraries always know exactly what they are doing and why, and that, of course, is why they are so large, are so successful, and are leaders in both the philosophy and practice of public librarianship.

The two libraries listed gave their highest priority to "popular materials library," and their lowest to "Research Center." If you look at all the other libraries of whatever size that reported that they have selected roles according to the PLA manual, you will find almost the same story.

Frankly, I'm encouraged here, mightily encouraged, on several counts. First, the work of the New Standards Task Force to delineate and publish the roles and the manual to determine these roles has had effect in the real world of public libraries themselves – something that is highly unusual for anything published by ALA, where guidelines and recommendations have a penetrating percentage in the profession of something on the order of 10 percent, I would guess.

Second, almost all public libraries have picked the "popular materials library" as their number-one role, which is exactly how they are used by the public almost everywhere.

Third, almost every library (the exceptions are interesting in themselves) has picked "Research Center" as third and lowest priority.

Fourth, someone out there had to be thinking about the whole business of roles and priorities, and that – thinking about it – may very well start the revolution in public libraries.

The other roles vary all over the lot in priorities, and I think that's inevitable and quite right, if you are going to design your service to meet your community's needs. Role identification, even if very carefully done and in accordance with the PLA Manual, is not, and cannot be, however, an end in itself. "The most common of all follies is to believe passionately in the palpably not true. It is the chief occupation of mankind" (H.L. Mencken).

I'm afraid that, although most public libraries are adopting as their first and most important role that of a "popular materials library," that does not describe the way they assign their resources, that's not the way they think, and that's not the way they operate. It is very, very difficult to question conventional wisdom all across the board, but to, in truth, operate a library that has the "popular materials library" as even *one* of the first two priorities, many public libraries will have to change dramatically.

This unwillingness to recognize that a public library has to be truly user-oriented, rather than institution-oriented, and must engage in truly consumer-oriented library planning *and* library operation is the most significant conflict in public library philosophy today. We have become fat, happy, and contented with a philosophy of operation that is academically oriented, elitist, suspicious, and contemptuous of ordinary people. We fanatically defend a system that serves our interests, rather than those of the people who provide the money to pay us, justifying all our actions by referring to the "public good," which of course is defined by us, not by the users.

I can, and often do, give endless examples of this kind of thinking in our profession, but I am beginning to think that most of our ineptitude comes down to one chilling fact: We don't know what we're doing; we don't analyze from the consumer point of view; and, what's worse, we *reject* the consumer point of view when it comes to our most important management responsibility, which is stock management. (Remember, I have stopped using the term *collection!*)

"Idealism is fine, but as it approaches reality, the cost becomes prohibitive" (William C. Buckley, Jr.). The clearest example of this kind of thinking, the one example that I give most often, and the one almost universally rejected by the conventional wisdom is the very existence of the central library. Without going into the myriad details that illustrate the inherent folly of the central library syndrome, let me just say that the real reason they were built in the first place and continue to expand is the warehouse function – the bigger the stock, the "better" the library, the more valuable and important you are to the public. The continuation of the myth is illustrated not only by building more and more of these disastrous money eaters in Chicago ($140 million), Memphis and Phoenix ($40 million each), San Francisco, and so on, but by insidious mottos like that promulgated by ALA: "Books worth reading are books worth saving."

Wonderful idealism. But let me tell you a secret: We can't afford it; we couldn't ever afford it; and we won't be able to afford it in the future, not without killing library service to the library's public, which is given most effectively and most efficiently in the community library or the branch library in the case of systems.

Central libraries not only store books (the responsibility of libraries, sure, but not *public* libraries) that the public library consumer no longer cares about and is unlikely to want in the future, but also supply at great expense the very specialized services, such as rare book rooms or special collections, which only a very small percentage of people ever use. Of course, this kind of library feeds the egos of the director and the trustees, but in every case – and I mean *every* case, it does this at the expense of service, attention, and worst of all, the supply of materials to the community libraries. There is just so much money to be spent on libraries, and librarians, politicians, and architects conspire to rob the community library of the resources necessary for stock development and staffing in the public's library, the community library.

There is no logical defense – hear me, no defense! – for the continuation of the construction of these monuments to intellectual vanity, and yet we continue to do so. What's more expensive and more destructive is that we continue to operate existing facilities in the face of all logical fiscal and rational proof to the contrary, fostered in this path by facile editorial writers in and out of the profession and politicians who have quite defensible agenda quite opposite and damaging to library service, and worst of all, ourselves. There is, I'm sure, a method of dismantling the unneeded, unused, but horribly expensive services and book-collecting mania of central libraries without the romantics and the elite noticing the dismantling and screaming. That shouldn't take a lot of scheming by a good manager, backed by a board interested in the public good, the *real* public good!

Enough about the conflict in public library roles that exist. What are we to do to eliminate the conflicts in our perceptions and in the public's perceptions about the role of public libraries in the community? This role, incidentally, should stand on its own merits, not on the merits of other kinds of libraries that serve specific segments of the public, instead of the multiple segments that constitute our consumer base.

As I have said, most of this comes down to stock management on behalf of our customers, the kind of management that successful companies use to increase their profits and the kind of management that will increase our value to those who support us and will increase the use of public libraries so that they will become major, not the present minor, contributors to quality of life.

Remember what I said about PLA's abandonment of quantitative standards? And the restiveness that still hasn't vanished about this abandonment? Nancy Bolt was right when she said librarians wanted standards.

I have here a list of standards, which if intelligently implemented in accordance with the differing demands of an individual community, will ensure that the public library will be resuscitated. The standards are pretty simply stated. Although most of them will prove somewhat difficult to implement in a traditional public library, believe me, it'll be worth it in the long run. The long run in this case will be about five years at the minimum, but results are guaranteed. These standards, developed by a blue-ribbon committee and based on years and years of public library experience, do not address every facet of public library management. They are broken down into general categories, with some, but not exhaustive, description to follow.

Stock Management (Formerly Collection Development)

Lets discuss eight elements of stock management.

1. Allot 20 Percent of Budget for Materials.

This is very, very difficult and very, very important. According to PLDS, the average percentage allotted to materials from the operating budget by American public libraries is 15 percent. You will also recognize that the ones who budget less than 10 percent are those with fiscal or management troubles. They don't have a reputation for excellence, but that's a general, not a specific, statement. In any event, 20 percent of materials will mean *less* for everything else, and different communities have different budget requirements year by year. But if you can average 20 percent for materials over a five-year period, you will have a better library, even if it is, perhaps, dirtier, more tattered, or more shortstaffed. The public will appreciate it – and *that* is what is important, not gleaming corridors!

2. Have No Central Library.

This is difficult to implement if you already have a central library. If you reorganize and despecialize the central library and weed the dickens out of it, you will be able to transfer resources, staff, and attention to your community libraries. *That's* where the taxpayers are!

If you have only *one* library, you don't have a central library. If you have branches that together circulate only a fraction of the circulation of the central library, you really don't have a "central library" within this definition, either.

If you have just passed a $40 million bond issue for a central library, invest the money. This will give you $3.2 million to add to your materials budget, exceeding standard 1 above. Congratulations.

3. Limit Stock to 200,000 Items in Any One Building.

No matter what the size of your community, never put more than 200,000 items, including books, videos, CDs, tapes, and periodical titles, in one building. Never. No excuse. If your community is larger than can be served by this building, build another. Users of public libraries are confused by too many books. This standard, together with the standard 1 above will force weeding. There is a very useful standard for that, too, but the blue-ribbon committee is keeping it secret until you can prove you need it.

Of course, stock under 200,000 is absolutely permitted and encouraged, depending on the size of your community. Stock under 10,000 and you no longer have a full-service library; you have a minilibrary.

4a. Organize Central Selection.

Don't waste time on materials selection. I didn't say don't *spend* time; just don't *waste* it. This means that a multiple-agency system should do central selection. The time of librarians serving the public is too precious to waste on duplicating 80 percent of the selections made by the 8,000+ public libraries in the country. Allied with this standard is the importance of speed. High-demand titles should be on shelves no more than three days later than at the bookstores. Lower-demand titles should be on public shelves no later than two weeks after receipt. It can be done.

If you are an independent library, get together with other libraries and have a gang of people select, order, and process the books. This is not possible economically without giving up your selection prerogative to someone else. Do it. You already have given someone else the *publishing* prerogative.

This standard will save public libraries $100 million annually in staff time to spend on standard 1 above. Congratulations on faster purchases.

4b. Practice Prepublication Ordering for 60-70 Percent of Titles.

This, along with standard 4a, will make sure that you get titles before they go out of print and that they will be on the shelves within three days of the bookstores, and it will still allow the selectors to see most new children's books, the general exception to this rule. Speed and currency are less important for children. Replacement of old goodies is.

5. Observe the 10,000-title Maximum Annually.

No library school professor, consultant, or professional association has ever to my knowledge addressed the issue of how many titles any public library of a given size should add to its stock annually. As a matter of experience, I have been shocked to discover that relatively few library directors know this statistic in their own libraries, and some library administrative staff even confuse titles with volumes! The number of titles purchased each year affects almost every cost and service measurement a library makes – or doesn't make, in some cases. Through experimentation over many years, the blue-ribbon committee has found that 10,000 titles, counting books and audiovisual items, will serve about 90 percent of the population of a million people 90 percent of the time. Buying more titles, given the same materials budget, will reduce the number of copies of these titles, making the most-wanted titles scarcer on the shelves, and will raise costs astronomically for cataloging, acquisitions, selection, shelving, storage, and many other ways. If you buy, say, 15,000 titles, you may satisfy 93 percent of the public instead of just 90 percent, but at what cost? This is a simple matter of inventory control to any well-run business, but an almost foreign concept to many of us in public libraries

Obviously, smaller public libraries should buy fewer titles according to size and type of population, but this standard should not be exceeded by practically any public library of any size for titles in English, except for special circumstances, of which I can't think of many. Publishers will abhor this standard.

6. Keep the Number of Titles in Any One Library Building at 40-50 Percent of the Number of Items.

In any community library–under these standards all public libraries are community libraries–your title count should be no more than 40-50 percent of your item count, except perhaps in special circumstances, such as failure to achieve a 20 percent level for your materials budget. This percentage will occur almost automatically if you spend a lot of money buying the titles that 90 percent of the users want, and it will also guarantee a higher level of duplication, which all research shows is more important than the number of titles. It will also force deselection, or weeding, as will the following standard.

7. Keep the Average Age of the Items (Not the Titles) in the Collection At Five Years.

People like new books, or at least attractive books in good condition with information that is not outdated. Few books in public libraries over five years old meet these requirements, and users respond by not borrowing them. This will mean, of course, that your collection, which will be designed of a size to match your community, will never get too old, that your old bestsellers and radio repair books will get deselected promptly according to a well thought out procedure, and that classics will be promptly replaced by new copies (classics are classics because they are read and worn out!). This is arguably the most important standard. Being a realist, however, I recognize that few libraries will be able to bring themselves to implement this practice, and they will be supported by their trustees, their staff, and the public, to whom discarding books is almost as unpopular as burning the flag. Publishers, however, will love this standard, as will Baker and Taylor.

8. Keep Your Stock Turnover Rate at 4 to 6.

Unless you select the titles the public wants, *not* the ones you want them to read, all your efforts will go for nothing. In other words, it isn't enough to buy materials. They have to be the *right* materials for the public you serve. That's not all that easy to determine, especially when you have to guess the number of copies of a title to buy. There are all sorts of methods and techniques to obtain the management information you need, especially now that we have circulation computers in many libraries, but the informed professional selector is still the key to success in this matter, with the emphasis in selection on what the *user* wants, not on what the librarian wishes to put on the shelves. This attitude – we are responsive rather than instructive – is not easy to find in this profession.

The key is to watch your turnover. If it isn't between 4 and 6 annually as an *average* for the whole collection, suspect that something is wrong. Maybe it's your selection.

If it's *over* 6, maybe you don't have enough copies of some of the titles. The rule is here: Pay attention to the public, pay attention to what they are borrowing, not what they *say* they are borrowing or will borrow but what they actually do.

Programming

In programming, there is only one standard to follow.

1. Program for Children Only.

Programming book talks, story hours, and so on is vital for preschoolers and grade schoolers. They are an absolute waste of time for everyone from middle school on up, including adults. Don't do it unless you are overstaffed or underworked or the mayor's wife just loves her Great Books Discussion.

If you are meeting most of these standards, you will be so busy that you won't have time for programming anyway, except for the children and perhaps the children's caregivers, who are increasingly important in influencing the use of library materials.

This of course means avoiding the National Endowment for the Humanities like the plague. It's a tremendous amount of work and expense for the number of people who participate, and most of the grant goes to college professors, not to the library.

Some programming, like pretty much all interlibrary loan, must be for political purposes – just know why you're doing it. Politics generally pays off; programming doesn't.

Buildings and Equipment

Follow these three standards on buildings and equipment.

1. Set Maximum Size for Any Library Building at 40,000 Square Feet.

Buildings are siren songs for librarians, politicians, and architects. For the politicians and architects, three-dimensional things are their lifeblood. Community libraries seldom, if ever, need more than 40,000 square feet, and most of the time they need considerably fewer. Three-fourths of the space should be public service space. This, of course, ties into standard 3; and standard 2 prohibits your central library,

If you have a system needing central administrative offices, put them in the basement of a shopping center so there'll be plenty of parking and shoe stores and restaurants for the central office staff. It's okay to put them in the shopping center office tower so the staff will have windows. Always keep the director away from the actual books. He or she will start special collections every time!

2. Use No Steel Bracket or Case Shelving – Only Shelving That Can Shelve Books Face Out and Spine Out.

Almost all public libraries have steel bracket or wood case shelving. Both are for storage, not for merchandizing books and other materials – and that's the business we're in. You use bracket shelving only for storage of seasonal materials (you shouldn't store anything else) out of sight of the public. Use display shelving for public-area stacks and everywhere else, like the bookstores. They may take more space, but it's worth it. Besides, more books will be out, so you won't have to have shelf space for them!

3. Know That Parking is More Important Than Location.

Wheeler was right in 1930; he's wrong in 1990. Even in cities, people drive a lot, and in suburbs and towns, nobody walks; they drive.

Parking is a greater determinant for library use than any other single factor. Ballard may be wrong about some things, but when he says you don't have to be in a shopping center or downtown, he's right. Even in the middle of a residential area is fine, if you have parking. If you don't, you're dead. Never settle for any site without plenty of easy, preferably free parking. Have parking, even if it costs.

Management

There are two standards for management.

1. Make a Long-range Plan Every Five Years.

If you don't know where you're going, any road will take you there. You've heard a lot about planning recently. Believe it. Involve the staff. A bad plan is better than no plan. At least it makes you think about what your library is doing. Or not doing.

2. Budget at Least 2 Percent of Personnel Costs for Staff Development.

Maybe this should be 3 percent to 5 percent. The blue-ribbon committee is still discussing this. It's amazing what we all can learn from the continuing education process, whether it's in-service, seminars, or professional conferences. This kind of thing, despite the ill-informed complaints of some taxpayers and appropriating authorities, does wonders for innovation, new skills, good attitude, morale, and low staff turnover. The academic librarians are generally encouraged in this area with funds; public librarians are discouraged, which is very shortsighted. Maybe the figure should be 4 percent for staff development. It's money well spent.

Staff

Follow these two standards.

1. Make One Half of Your Librarians Paraprofessionals.

It's crazy to think that you need to have an MLS to do all professional tasks in a library. For management and training, yes. For information desk work, no. You'll be able to recruit good college graduates who are not yet ready, perhaps, to commit to librarianship as a career but who are capable people, with some careful training. A secret: There are thousands of these people in the profession doing a good job with users. Why ALA hasn't gone after them always surprises me. Paraprofessionals have other advantages, too, such as good contacts in the local community.

2. Make All Public Service Librarians Generalists.

Actually, nearly all public service librarians are generalists because the smaller libraries can't afford specialists. Neither can the new poor, the large libraries who are spending so much for their central libraries that they can't hire enough librarians to keep up the fiction of specialization. Anyway, why can't all of our librarians be trained to do everything? I know some may not like it. As human beings and as products of our educational system, we *like* being specialists.

There's a lot of argument about generalists, but most of it has to do with status of librarians, not with service to the public. This standard is already fulfilled, but not admitted, in 95 percent of the nation's libraries. We should recognize it and train our staff for it.

Conclusion

These standards, if adhered to generally, will ensure that many of the role conflicts, which are either real or perceived in American's libraries, will be eliminated or greatly reduced. This does not mean, of course, that the successful adoption of a true public library role will solve all our problems.

We will continue to have problems with funding and staffing, and we will have general administrative and managerial challenges of all kinds. But if we clearly delineate the mission and role of the public library so that it is really the *public's* library, we will be prepared to face the major changes that the next decade will bring to the fore: issues such as the effect of online information and full-text printing on present book collecting and book-saving practice. This promises to be the real death knell for large central libraries. The fee or free issue will be resolved, I am sure, in favor of limited fees but will have a major impact on public library funding.

But all that's another story contained in a clouded crystal ball.

Note

1. Stephen Apey, "McLibraries," *New Republic* 202, no. 9 (26 February 1990): 12.

Public Library Effectiveness

ELEANOR JO RODGER

Executive Director
Public Library Association
American Library Association
Chicago, Illinois

> We should be a bit wary of the little library right in the middle of the country. For when it is good, it is very, very good. And when it is bad . . . it's a pretty good library for a town this size.

In lay language, the most frequent assessment of public library effectiveness is this last phrase, "a pretty good library for a town this size." In this essay, I will talk about public library effectiveness and flesh out a bit the concept of a pretty good library. I will share a thought or two about how we can get from pretty good public libraries to effective public libraries.

Thinking about "Effectiveness"

The literature on organizational effectiveness, OE as it is known, is helpful in providing ways to organize the various dimensions of public library effectiveness. I would like to briefly lay these out, relate them to public librarianship, and explain how I believe we have the managerial tools at our disposal to create the best of all possible worlds. Then I'd like to move to a discussion of one facet of public library effectiveness that I believe is absolutely crucial if we are to thrive, not merely survive, and then quickly discuss central libraries and their potential contribution to effectiveness.

In the literature review section of *The Public Library Effectiveness Study*,[1] Tom Childers and Nancy Van House helpfully distill four approaches to organizational effectiveness, drawn chiefly from the work of Kim Cameron. They are as follows:

1. The *goal* or *rational systems approach* assumes organizations are effective when they achieve their goals. Librarians can assume they are effective if they broaden their base, increase circulation, develop an information center for government officials, or whatever else they may have intended to do. The effective public library accomplishes what it plans to do.

2. The *process* or *natural systems model* assumes organizations are effective when organizational equilibrium is maintained, organizational health thrives, and internal processes are sound. This treatment of effectiveness values things such as high staff morale, low turnover, and consistent procedures. The effective public library is perceived as a good place to work.

3. Organizations must acquire resources from their environment. The *open systems or system resource model* of effectiveness evaluates organizations based on their success in acquiring needed resources. Using this dimension, an effective public library is one that manages to acquire and maintain adequate funding, political support, and community prestige.

4. Finally, the literature tells us, organizations must meet the needs and expectations of strategic constituencies. This is known as the *multiple constituencies* or *participant satisfaction model* of effectiveness. Strategic contingencies for public libraries usually include users, trustees, friends, and often the community's business and education leaders. Historically, we have had less challenge in the area because constituents' expectations of public libraries have been high in generalities and low in specifics

Fortunately, we do not have to choose among these approaches to organizational effectiveness. They each measure different aspects of our efforts. Putting them all together, we can summarize by saying that the effective public library is one that is well funded, achieves its goals, has high staff morale, and has pleased all the right people. It's hard to quarrel with that!

Unlike Charles Robinson, I have no silver bullet formula to offer to make this happen. I do believe, however, that the book *Planning and Role Setting for Public Libraries* gives our profession a splendid resource for enhancing the possibility that our libraries, individually and collectively, will move in this direction. A library that has thoughtfully completed the "Planning to Plan" and "Looking Around" stages of the process will have meaningfully involved staff and will have identified key stakeholders, thereby addressing key components of the natural systems and multiple constituencies models of effectiveness. After selecting roles, they will have developed goals, objectives, and strategies to focus the library's resources. As the plan gets implemented, objectives will be achieved, making the library successful in the rational systems dimension. There are, of course, no guarantees that responsive, focused libraries run by happy staff will attract and sustain community support and funding, but the chances of it are greater than they are for unresponsive, diffuse institutions staffed by grumpy folks.

The Crucial Factor of Effectiveness

To make public libraries good, we have to make them easy to use. This has not been our custom. We have traditionally opened libraries at hours librarians like to work, rather than when the public has discretionary time. We have required people to be familiar with our notions about the organization of knowledge to find items or answers, or they must find librarians to ask. We rarely provide adequate parking. We store materials on the same subject in a minimum of five different places in the building.

An article by Jeffrey Prottas of Harvard in the *Public Administration Review* almost ten years ago, entitled "The Cost of Free Services: Organizational Impediments to Access to Public Services,"[2] organized my scattered discontent about our crucial access problems in public libraries.

When organizations can't or don't charge for their outputs, Prottas says, demand quickly outstrips supply–assuming, of course, they are putting out a product or service people want. One (unintentional, I believe) way libraries have faced this dilemma is to have some services and materials nobody wants.

It is, of course, appropriate for public policy makers and public administrators to develop ways to limit free services. Initially, limiting participation in free public services is done by carefully developing statements of eligibility. Only residents of Evanston can use this beach or library. Only persons who make less than $15,000 can use this health clinic. All residents of Maryland can use this public library.

If the excess demand issues remain after eligibility requirements are met, there are three organizational levels at which actions are taken to increase user costs as a conscious or an unconscious strategy for closing the gaps between demand and supply.

At the policy level of organizations, structure and funding are decided. Most of this is done for public libraries by cooperative actions taken by boards and top administrators. Here are some examples. It is a policy/funding issue to not be open Sunday. The user cost is to make time to come to the library after work. It is a policy issue to not answer homework questions on the telephone. The user cost is a trip to the library. It is a policy question to decide to spend 10 percent of the budget on materials. The user cost is to wait for a copy from interlibrary loan or until a reserve copy becomes available.

Many more user costs are added at the administrative or procedure level. In our not so recent past this meant limits on the number of books that could be checked out at once. Now it may mean limits on the number of videos, shortened circulation times for high-demand materials, a waiting period before a library card is issued, or preregistration for children's story hours. Procedures that limit services are necessary, and they are part of good administration as long as they are congruent with the governing body's policies. Often they aren't.

The representative of institutional authority most likely to encounter the client in any public service is the "street-level bureaucrat," the person either who controls access to the service or who actually provides it. In public libraries, street-level bureaucrats are any and all persons who work at public service desks or who walk about public service areas shelving books, straightening magazines, or organizing displays. As Prottas notes, "The street-level bureaucrat can vary enormously the pleasantness of attempting to obtain a service. Naturally clients are not without resources of their own in the encounter, but the street-level bureaucrat clearly has the upper hand because the applicant is under enormous pressure to conform to the agency's expectations in order to receive the desired service."[3]

If services are not properly limited or "focused" by policy and implementation procedures, the street-level bureaucrat finds himself or herself engaging in behaviors that may inappropriately raise the user's cost of obtaining services. Harassed reference librarians who point vaguely to a distant shelf instead of going with patrons to see if needed material is there, circulation staff who busy themselves with filing chores avoiding answering patrons' questions, and children's librarians who schedule preschool story hours during preschoolers' naptime are all limiting access to library resources because of real or perceived work overload, rather than implementing policies.

Other observations Prottas makes that are relevant to library service include:

- Long delays in obtaining service impose a time cost on the user.

- Suppression of information raises real and perceived costs. Potential users must know enough about the benefits of service to invest the time to apply for them.

- The poor, the elderly, and the disabled are most strongly dissuaded from program participation by high time or money costs of travel.

- Applicants are often excluded from services because they lack the necessary skills to apply.

- Decisions not to market public services strike hardest at clients who are isolated from informal networks.

- Street-level rationing raises the price of service and lowers its value more for uninformed than for informed citizens.

Let me repeat – rationing free services is not a bad thing. It must be done, but it is appropriately done at the policy level, not at the implementation level. If a library decides that its primary roles are as a popular materials library and a formal education support center for elementary and middle school children, it need not schedule preschool story hours at inconvenient times hoping no one will come; it can simply not have any. A library selecting primary roles as a reference center and a community activities center need not apologize for a four-week delay in getting bestsellers into the hands of readers. Fast delivery of bestsellers is not the focus of their resource allocation.

Once a library board decides on its mission and roles, however, it *must* make its resources and services easy to use. Libraries that are easy will be used. Libraries that aren't won't be. A public library that isn't used isn't effective, no matter how many professional verbal flags we wrap it in. Public libraries that are so badly led and managed that they are not heavily used are not democracy's resource or democracy's anything.

I have a few general thoughts to share on making libraries easier to use. Most are obvious, but just in case, here they are.

1. Get rid of signage that assumes people know or care about the Dewey decimal system. Replace it with natural language signage. If you must have numbers for pages or for the 14 percent of public library patrons doing known-item searches, make the numbers small and put them under other signs.

2. Keep your library open at least 20 hours a week during the times your target audiences have discretionary time.

3. Offer reference services to businesses and fax-to-fax communication. It's probably cheaper than face-to-face.

4. If you can't figure out how to have drive-in stations to circulate books, at least provide them for book returns, despite the snowballs in the book drop and all that.

5. Consider letting patrons buy extensions on loan periods ahead of time rather than fining them for not reading faster and keeping books too long.

6. As any change in practice or procedure is considered, do a "user impact statement." If the change adds to the users' costs of obtaining the service in any way incongruent with library policy, don't do it!

7. Reward staff for thinking up ways to make library use easier for the public, not for simply showing up or thinking of ways to save money.

We are probably not yet at the professional point of having staff wear badges that say, "Ask me. I'm easy," but I hope we're closer to the day when we can have bumper stickers that say, "Life – Librarians Make It Easier."

Central Libraries

In "Conflicting Roles in the Public Library," Charles Robinson has so strongly recommended that we abolish central libraries. I do not share his belief that the term effective central libraries is an oxymoron.

In a nutshell – and this is not an ad hominem attack – he objects to the fact that central libraries drain needed resources from community libraries because nobody uses them. He does, however, concede that they are politically useful in jurisdictions with something like a city center. I share his opposition to wasted resources. I do not share his conviction that there is a one-to-one equation between central libraries and resource waste. I do agree with Bill Summers's 1984 assessments that "The central library developed to serve a particular kind of city, and that city has either passed or is passing away," and that "Of the functions that central libraries have traditionally carried out, many are no longer necessary or can be conducted as well or better in alternative spaces at far less cost."[4]

Central libraries appear to be enduringly important to politicians; politicians are enduringly important to public libraries; and most urban areas have both already and are unlikely to abandon them. It seems appropriate, then, that we reinvent central libraries so that money spent on the buildings and services provided in them can contribute to the fulfillment of each particular library's mission and to the glory of the politicians who control key purse strings.

We do not need to house large retrospective library collections in the city's high-rent district, if we public librarians need to store them at all. We particularly do not need to store large retrospective collections of children's literature in children's rooms in center cities where there are few children or kiddie lit researchers. We do not need to house technical services, processing, delivery systems, or library administrators downtown. What do we really need in the downtown library?

The answer partially depends on the nature of the downtown. Some cities die by seven o'clock each evening. Some have active residential and entertainment use well into the evening. Almost all have active business and governmental communities during the day. Central libraries can and should serve the people who live and work downtown and those suburban and out-of-town visitors who will come downtown to see and do things not available elsewhere. Having relocated the retrospective collections and support services, we now have huge amounts of room for new or expanded uses. Some suggestions, many not novel, include:

- A community library for the urban community.

- A business center with information services augmented by other business support services, offered for a fee.

- *Many* quiet reading, listening, and viewing areas.

- Conference rooms and classrooms.

- Shopping referral services.

- Bookstore/café space where book lovers could hang out, converse, and think.

- A visitors center where newcomers, tourists, and others could learn about the city's past and present.

- A "citizen's advice bureau," modeled on the British institution, where residents could find out about and have initial access to all city services.

- An auditorium for concerts, speeches, political debates, and the like.

- A job and career testing, counseling, and information center to provide support for the three to five career changes most adults will make.

- Subject-specific information "boutiques" featuring materials in all formats relative to the particular subject area. The food information boutique, for example, might include recipes and nutrition books, magazines, online restaurant reviews and reservations booking, and ingredient and equipment shopping information. The medical information boutique would feature access to Medline, books and magazines on health and illness, computerized access to local doctor and hospital information and to medical self-help groups.

- PARKING – SAFE AND CONVENIENT.

The challenge before us is not to struggle politically to rid ourselves of central libraries, but to work with elected officials and urban leaders to reinvent them to serve our cities and the people who live and work there.

Conclusion

Rene Dubos quotes Andre Gide's admonition to create of oneself "the most unique, and irreplaceable of beings" by saying those things only *we* can say and by doing those things only *we* can do. I believe this is our professional challenge – to create effective, unique, and irreplaceable public libraries by assessing with vision and with care what we uniquely can be in our communities and what we can do for them – and then we must do it with enthusiasm, clarity, and superb management. Our communities deserve it. Our role in society demands it.

Notes

1. Thomas Childers and Nancy A. Van House, *The Public Library Effectiveness Study: Final Report* (Philadelphia: Drexel University College of Information Studies, 1989).

2. Jeffrey Manditch Prottas, "The Cost of Free Services: Organizational Impediments to Access to Public Services," *Public Administration Review*, September/October 1981, 526-34.

3. Ibid., 528.

4. F. William Summers, "Alternatives to the Central Library," *Public Libraries*, Spring 1984, 4-7.

PART 4
Samuel Lazerow Memorial Lecture

Samuel Lazerow Memorial Lecture: The National Legislative Agenda

GARY E. STRONG

State Librarian
State Library of California
Sacramento, California

As the tanks bore down on the students in Tiananmen Square, my heart was heavy. The gun fire took the precious lives of those struggling to gain freedom of expression and thought. When the Berlin Wall began to crack, my heart was filled with hope and exhilaration. Freedom broke through. The cracks became great openings allowing free choice. One heard the words *freedom* and *choice* spoken loudly and without shame. We are reminded that we take for granted our freedoms and tenants of democracy.

A friend of mine recently took the oath to become a United States citizen. For him, the treasure of freedom is so real—nothing is more precious. His struggle to escape Vietnam, the danger of the crowded boat, the ordeal of a refugee camp, the waiting for word that he could come to America, the hunger, and the boredom make his freedom even more precious.

Will we in libraries be able to meet the challenge of freedom in the twenty-first century? Will libraries play a role in the future? Will libraries be able to preserve the past for reflection in the future? Will libraries find the resources to continue to make a difference in people's lives?

What must our national library legislative agenda be if we are to survive? I hope I can set a bit of the stage for that agenda, rather than provide a pat formula filled with answers and opinions.

One of the first tasks of the Bush administration was to convene the President's Summit on Education. The president and the governors agreed to:

- Establish a process for setting national education goals.

- Seek greater flexibility and enhanced accountability in the use of federal resources to meet the goals through both regulatory and legislative changes.

- Undertake a major state-by state effort to restructure our education system.

- Report annually on progress in achieving our goals.[1]

Several states have followed this conference with state-level conferences. I was invited to attend the Superintendent's Education Summit in California, but I was there to lead discussions on adult literacy, not on library service.

The actions on behalf of education in his first budget as president, however, leave much doubt as to Bush's real commitment. Following Reagan rhetoric, the Library Services and Construction Act (LSCA) has been targeted by the Department of Education through the budget process for virtual elimination. Because it was declared that the LSCA has served its purpose and that other priorities demand the funds, Titles I and II are zero funded. One of the reasons put forth is that little of the money goes directly to local libraries.

My own state was cited as being one of the states where a small percentage finds its way to local public libraries. This is just false and is, I believe, a result of the practices of reporting that rolls programs together for reporting purposes. In this process, the reports leave the impression that money does not reach the local library. In fact, more than 80 percent of California's Title I LSCA funding and 100 percent of our Title III funding goes to support local and regional library services.

At the same time as the president's education summit, Bush announced new initiatives to curb the increase in drug use. To support this initiative, he acted in a fashion that few could question. He "took" a percentage of each agency's budget right off the top to dedicate to the undeclared war on drugs.

Foreign affairs took dramatic and forceful new directions with the fall of the Berlin Wall and the opening of Eastern Europe. Promises of troop reductions and deployment of military spending have been offered. Domestic military expenditures are targeted for reduction. Lists of bases have been identified for closure, including many in my own state. Rhetoric abounds as this new administration takes control.

The Work of Congress

As we assess a possible strategy for a national legislative agenda for libraries, let us review the major issues that will face our national leaders during the next few years. Within Congress itself, issues of campaign finance, congressional pay, honoraria, and ethics investigations in both the Senate and House occupy much attention. The budget demands center stage for discussion along with the capital gains tax rate, new revenues for reaching the deficit target, the thrift bailout, review of stock market regulation, the trade deficit, and restrictions on trade with the Soviets.

As Congress reviews government and commerce, it will consider reauthorization of the Clean Air Act, revisions to farm programs, creation of legislation concerning oil-spill liability and compensation, regulation of pesticides, reauthorization of the Resource Conservation and Recovery Act, the logging of the Tongass National Forest, pension reversions, family and medical leave, and rural development. Congress is expected to reauthorize the Commodity Futures Trading Commission as well as crack down on futures trading abuse and propose legislation to limit the commercial content of children's television. The re-regulation of cable television is set for consideration. Airline leveraged buyouts and "Baby Bell" business restrictions will be examined along with changes to the fairness doctrine. NASA funding, technology programs, and Agent Orange will receive particular attention.

Within the arena of social policy, Congress will clear some type of child care legislation, provide more funds for antidrug efforts, and work to override the president on the status of Chinese students. Civil rights guarantees for the disabled, abortion, health care, and anticrime proposals will all call for action. The housing program is up for reauthorization in the midst of the HUD scandal. Legal immigration is an important issue to states like California and Florida. Legislation encouraging volunteerism will move along. Bush's education initiatives move the chairs around and will draw fire from groups like librarians. The Vocational Education Act is up for reauthorization.

Countering attention on domestic and national programs will be discussion of the defense budget, strategic arms agreements, the strategic defense initiative, and the strategic arms reduction treaty. Nicaragua, El Salvador, Eastern Europe, China, and South Africa will draw our attention. Demand on foreign aid will be stiff.[2]

All of these issues make it more difficult for librarians to articulate a national or federal policy with respect to library service. Plans for the White House Conference on Library and Information Services are well under way and states are rallying to create pre-White House Conference Activities that will select and prepare their delegates to be ready to do battle for states' interests in library and information services. Associations, libraries, and individuals have begun to position themselves with statements and declarations, hearings, and library rhetoric. Each of us responsible for planning and development of library services at the state level has attempted to decide how best to cope with this "opportunity" at the national level. Most, in point of fact, are comparing how well they did with respect to the 1979 White House conference. Much is speculated on how effective it was and what developments since can really be attributed to the actions and recommendations of that conference.

I was privileged to participate with 23 other library professionals in a process of defining federal roles in support of public library services. The results of our initial meeting in September 1989 have been widely disseminated, and hearings were held at the midwinter meeting of the American Library Association to take testimony of support and concern for the statements embodied in the paper resulting from the effort. The preamble of the document, "One Nation, 250 Million Individuals Public Library Services for a Diverse People the Roles of the Federal Government," succinctly states a purpose for a new look at the national legislative agenda. It begins: "We are a remarkable and rapidly changing country of 250 million people, strengthened by the involvement of our citizens, shaped by cultural diversity and individual initiative, and nurtured by a climate of freedom of mind, thought, and expression."

As the agenda of the White House Conference on Library and Information Services suggests, our future depends on a literate, learning population; a healthy economy; and effective participation on the part of all citizens. We face, however, some overriding national problems: illiteracy, drug abuse, homelessness, a diminishingly skilled work force, escalating health care costs, and conflicts generated by intolerance and misunderstanding. We also face new challenges: Older concepts of majority and minority cultures are becoming obsolete; the very notion of family itself is being redefined; rapidly changing technology is presenting both opportunities and barriers. We as a people need to act. We must deal with social problems involving requirements for equity and justice for an ethnically and culturally diverse population. Our education system cries out for attention. Solutions demand our best imagination, thinking, and leadership. Keys to solving our problems include valuing diversity, taking control of our lives, and creating coalitions to shape our future.[3]

You should carefully examine the recommendations of this paper and of others that will be completed for discussion prior to the White House conference. Along with issues identified from the states, these recommendations will form the locus of discussion at the conference now set for July 1991.

Recommendations for the National Agenda

If we are to succeed in our libraries, we must help in defining the national legislative agenda. This national agenda is not just for libraries, but for education and other domestic issues. We must carefully determine what the issues are and how libraries can position themselves to articulate their role in respect to the issues. I believe that the library response must fall into two arenas.

The first is the context of support to the administrative, resource, and management structures that are required to keep libraries healthy and successful. Most of the traditional federal programs of support fall into this category—for example, the interlibrary and networking components of the Library Services and Construction Act, the postal rate subsidy, depository programs of the Government Printing Office, catalog and bibliographic data from the Library of Congress, advocacy on the part of the National Commission for Libraries and Information Services, and similar programs. This list is the one that we generally create when asked to articulate the federal role with respect to library services.

Among the recommendations agreed upon by those of us meeting in Chicago last September and reaffirmed at the ALA midwinter meeting were the following:

1. That Congress reauthorize in 1994 the Library Services and Construction Act expanded and funded to reflect the critical needs of special populations and the employment of emerging technologies to link libraries more effectively with users.

2. That Congress continue, expand, and fund those federal programs that benefit public library users both directly and indirectly.[4]

It appears that there may be an uphill battle on our hands even before 1994. The Bush budget, as I mentioned, recommends a zero budget amount for LSCA Titles I and II. The administration's rhetoric justifying this recommendation is that only one-quarter of the LSCA funds reach the targeted population groups. We will have to fight hard this year to achieve the funding of the current program. While it appears that we have achieved the reauthorization of LSCA at this time, the future once again leaves us less than reassured that it will continue to be funded. In addition, I believe that we must keep LSCA a state-based program that responds to state-identified needs and concerns. I challenge my state library colleagues to work creatively to shift ongoing support for programs to state funds and to use LSCA funds to support new, innovative programs for the improvement of library services directly to people.

I believe there is another arena in which libraries must become more aggressive. This arena is one in which we will work in coalition with other organizations and institutions to influence change in public policy. Several examples illustrate these efforts. The Paperwork Reduction Act is a prime example of necessary coalition action. We cannot take on the private sector interests alone.

Again, we have recommended that two additional recommendations be considered.

3.　That Congress direct federal agencies to use the nationwide network of public libraries as well as the depository library system to disseminate information people need to address and solve critical national problems.

4.　That Congress allocate to public libraries a percentage of funds to address such pressing national concerns as drug abuse, literacy, youth at risk, and an aging population.[5]

Is the federal government ready to respond to these recommendations or to others that will be developed by other library groups and by the White House conference when it convenes in 1991? Congressman George Brown spoke of his concerns at a conference we sponsored several years ago now, and they ring true today. "And while I'm thrilled at the inexorable progress of our scientific and technological knowledge, I continue to be frustrated at our inability to control its impact and channel it to human benefit. . . You have to be something of an optimist to stay in this business, and I'm beginning to lose my optimism in terms of whether or not we can control this wonderful scientific and technological society which we are creating because I see this void in leadership, this vacuum, and I see so much of what we do and provide direction to, as being anti-human, aimed at destruction rather than creation. And that is the part that makes me pessimistic."[6]

He continues, "I perceive the failures may be rooted in the way in which our scientific and industrial society, modern man, organizes his knowledge, his culture, and his institutions. And that's a disturbing thought. We put a premium on individualistic, fragmented, reductionist approaches to all our problems. We are uncomfortable with holistic, integrated, humanistic solutions. In science this produces discipline and department oriented specialization. And of course remarkable fruitful research. In politics and in

Congress it produces fragmented, jurisdictional, interest group oriented approaches to all of our problems. We can no more bring coherence to an area which cuts across the jurisdiction of a half dozen Congressional committees, as information policy does, than we can . . . well, you name it."[7]

We are experiencing incredible change in California, a tidal wave of change that may exceed our coping ability. It may actually be getting out of control. Our old ways of thought, our institutions – they can all change, but the pace at which they can change may be too limited to meet the rapidity with which these new generations will be able to take advantage of our democracy.

"The federal government should focus more directly on the ability of the state library to provide leadership for library development in the respective states, continue to provide funding for innovative programs and service delivery, and develop the network of services available from all agencies of the federal government that allow state libraries to tap the information resources that they need to serve their primary clientele.

"A strong federal role and involvement for libraries will be the backbone of any national library network which is to develop. State library agencies are major hubs in that network and must work to insure the success of such national systems."[8]

These changes must focus on the effective use of technology and the linkages of that technology to allow us to communicate among ourselves more effectively. Further, the entry ports to this communication highway must allow for access by the end user in the research, governmental, corporate, and lay communities. These efforts will consume tremendous commitment and energy. Our challenge will be to balance the technology against the human factors and the values of library and information services.

I alluded earlier to the remarks of Congressman George Brown concerning the challenge of framing information policy at the federal level. With the growing use of technology by many sectors across the country, the continued struggle over access to government-produced information, international competition, and the need to protect intellectual property present tremendous challenges. Each of these areas of policy concern is an appropriate topic for full exploration in its own right. We cannot accomplish such a review here beyond identifying the areas as key information policy issues and suggesting that it will take involvement beyond the federal level to address them adequately.

The condition of our national libraries, including the Library of Congress, is alarming. Will we enter the next century with a continually crippled ability to lead the world in the realm of bibliographic standards and national access? The implications of not having access to the right information in the future are staggering. The arrearage at the Library of

Congress exceeds 38 million items. While some of this may not be earth-shattering, much of it is and deserves attention.

One of the key issues for the decade that we must all address is the needs of children in our society. This again is especially true for California. The reality faces us squarely. "Within the next generation, California's current population of children will grow from 8 million to more than 11 million. The demographic trends tell us that more and more of these children are at risk. There are increasing numbers of minority youth, decreasing numbers of two-parent families, and soaring numbers of children who can be categorized as poor or nearly poor. The trends all point to serious problems facing California's children."[9]

"The sheer number of children has an obvious impact on schools. By 1995 California's school enrollment will equal the total enrollment of this nation's 24 smallest states. State enrollment is currently growing by more than 150,000 pupils per year, more than the total enrollment of eight other states. Financing enrollment growth and cost-of-living adjustments alone will carve an additional $26 billion out of the state's budget in the next ten years. . ."[10]

We cannot ignore the children and young people of this nation who are at risk. We must be sure that these next generations are well prepared to lead our government, our corporations, our universities, our international relationships, our families, and our communities. A part of the national legislative agenda must concentrate on the children and youth of the nation – and it must be more than just talk.

Libraries and librarians must be a part of the crafting of solutions at all levels of government. The federal government must, however, set the stage and define its leadership role and do so quickly. The impact in my state of the loss of targeted funding for school libraries, for example, has been the serious erosion of school libraries. Without the promise of dedicated federal funds that are required to be spent on libraries, little state money is leveraged to support school libraries and media centers. This is the lesson we should learn about LSCA and the Higher Education Act. It may not be much money, but the funds leveraged at the state and local level are significant.

Anyone who knows me very well, knows of my interest in and concern about the condition of literacy in our nation. The national statistics are staggering. At least two in five adults in America today do not have the necessary level of literacy skills to read at a basic survival level. I could recount the horror stories that I have heard from people who have been served by our library literacy program. The self-empowerment about which they speak is wonderful.

We are finally seeing a national attention to this challenge. I give much credit to ABC/PBS for its Project Literacy US (PLUS), the Business Council for Effective Literacy, and Barbara Bush. Mrs. Bush spent a morning with us recently to celebrate the success of several of our new readers. Her presence and support drew the press, but her warmth won the people. New readers and their tutors felt her sincere interest and concern about them, their stories, their families, and their success. She is a wonderful champion for reading – and after all, I still believe libraries are all about reading.

As the national response is crafted through the Sawyer bill and like legislation, we in libraries must be sure that benefits are derived by library literacy programs, not just by adult education, job training, and other such program interests aimed at the economy and the workplace. Someone must be standing up and screaming loudly about the value of reading and the value of reading skills to the individual person. People must benefit first in their daily lives. They will in turn benefit the workplace and their community.

National Research and Education Network (NREN)

The United States is facing a serious challenge to its leadership both economically and technologically. The research and education that drive the American economy have led the world in prestige and results, but that lead is being threatened and is now eroding. The coalition for the Educational Research and Education Network has advocated that the "United States government, business and industry, and education are falling behind because they cannot access the information resources they need to stay ahead. The coalition maintains that if the United States fails to make it possible for researchers and educators to effectively use its information resources, this country can no longer lead the world in new ideas and innovation, and we will be unable to provide the technological training necessary to function effectively in a global economy. They propose the creation of the National Research and Education Network that can be the information superhighway of tomorrow.

NREN is conceived as a high-capacity, state-of-the-art computer network that could link supercomputers, libraries, national databases, and academic and industrial researchers into a unified information infrastructure. Turning information resources into building blocks for increasing industrial productivity will create new products and improve access to education and to information. We are indeed in an international, global marketplace. We must respond. Perhaps the National Research and Education Network can bring libraries and researchers and education together to take advantage of the tremendous resources that we have gathered together.

This is only one example of what challenges libraries will face in the use of telecommunications in the next decade. The coalitions that we are able to build with others who are interested and concerned about the impact of deregulation will be important players in our institutional empowerment.

These discussions may be further complicated by the possible entry of the telephone companies into the information generation arena. I can assure you that their motivation is profit, not service or access to information for all people.

We are faced today with a shrinking availability of federal government information. We must take positive steps toward ensuring that the information collected, generated, and owned by government at various levels shall always be available through our system of public access. Much credit is due to the Washington Office of the American Library Association for its steadfast support and position on access to government information. We must take issue with the reduction of access to government information.[11] I am astonished that more professors and researchers have not joined librarians in decrying this situation. It is an affront to academic freedom and to university supported research and development.

The 1990 census will be a pivotal point in access to government information. The completeness, accuracy, and analysis of these data collected will determine the allocation of federal funds as well as the composition of the House of Representatives. The release of data from these files to support local, regional, and state planning in states as complex as California and Florida is crucial to future planning efforts.

We all know how much effort and capital it takes to integrate technology into library services. Automation of a library is often a multiyear process that requires training, retraining, extensive public relations, redirection of funds, and continued retrofitting as a library moves through the process.

As we address the changing demographics of this nation in terms of its ethnic and racial complexion as well as its element of aging, we must recognize that change in library service and structures will take no less effort than automation or, in fact, any other major change. We are becoming a global nation in all aspects of life.

We cannot count on traditional approaches and answers to keep libraries active participants in this change. In its study of the public library response to changing populations, completed last year, the RAND Corporation suggested that the basic mission of libraries, to serve all Californians very well, may need to be reexamined given the limitation of funding available to libraries.

I believe that this is the same attack being forged at the national level. Rather than supporting and seeking change and standing ready to assist, the federal government is getting out of the business of serving people and helping those institutions that do. We must call for a revitalization of research in library and information science issues.

I believe that we will have to actively continue to examine the federal role with respect to libraries. We may lose federal support for libraries if the rhetoric is allowed to continually chip away at the fabric of our mission. While the value of information and its creation will be high, the value of those institutions that have traditionally collected, organized, housed, and provided access to ideas and knowledge will lose ground.

We must continue to speak out loudly at the national level. You do so first by clearly understanding the purpose and value of library service. You do so by articulating those values in your work. You participate by understanding the issues and acting on them in the ballot box. You do so by having opinions and by expressing them in the act of public discourse. As librarians, I believe we together can set the national legislative agenda for libraries and that we can influence that broader agenda for education. We must for the sake of our children and their children. Yes, I believe there is a role for the federal government concerning libraries.

Notes

1. Office of Educational Research and Improvement, Library Programs, January 1990.

2. *Congressional Quarterly Weekly Report,* 6 January 1990.

3. "One Nation, 250 Million Individuals, Public Library Services for a Diverse People: The Roles of the Federal Government. Twenty-four Library Leaders Ask You to Read this Document – and React to It – at Midwinter," *American Libraries,* December 1989, 1104.

4. Ibid.

5. Ibid.

6. Robert M. Hayes, ed., *Libraries and the Information Economy of California,* A conference sponsored by the California State Library (Los Angeles: GSLIS/UCLA, 1985), 69.

7. Ibid.

8. Gary E. Strong, "Impact of the Federal Government on State Library Services," in *State Library Services and Issues: Facing Future Challenges,* (Norwood, N.J.: Ablex Publishing Corporation, 1986), 61.

9. Karen Smith Thiel, "Children: Little Help for the Innocents," *California Journal,* January 1990, 47.

10. Michael Kirst, "Education: The Solution to California's Problems," *California Journal,* January 1990, 50.

11. American Library Association, Washington Office. *Less Access to Less Information, By and about the U.S. Government: A 1985-1989 Chronology* (Washington, D.C.: ALA, 1989).

PART 5
The Federal and State Legislative Agenda

Federal Legislation: Current and Developing

EILEEN D. COOKE

Director
ALA Washington Office
Washington, D.C.

The Library Services and Construction Act (LSCA) has a new five-year lease on life. The conference report reconciling the differences in the bill was passed by the House by a vote of 401 to 4 on 27 February 1990 and by an unanimous voice vote in the Senate on 1 March 1990. President Bush signed the five-year extension and amendments, HR 2742, into law on 15 March 1990. It is now Public Law 101-254.

LCSA Issues

During National Library Week Legislation Day in 1989 in Washington, D.C., many attended the joint House-Senate hearing on LSCA. It was a standing-room-only crowd of library supporters, and the House and Senate lawmakers seemed very favorably inclined to take prompt action on the legislation. Following the hearing, things seemed to move along in timely fashion with both House and Senate education subcommittees saying they would make minimal changes in the current law. They anticipated that the White House Conference on Library and Information Services (WHCLIS) process, generating recommendations from the grass roots–the folks back home–would give them a much better idea of what substantive changes should be made. These would reflect their constituents' needs for the next decade and on into the twenty-first century.

You can see the details of the latest version of LSCA by reading over the conference report in the *Congressional Record* for 27 February 1990, pp. H 444-8.

The principal provisions of the LSCA Amendments of 1990, specified in *House Report 101-407*, are:

- Title I Public Library Services: $100,000,000.

- Title II Public Library Construction and Technology Enhancement: $55,000,000.

- Title III Interlibrary Cooperation: $35,000,000.

- Title IV Indian Library Service: 2 percent of appropriations for I, II, III.

- Title V Foreign Language Materials: $1,000,000.

- Title VI Library Literacy Programs: $10,000,000.

- Title VII Evaluation and Assessment: $500,000.

- Title VIII Library Learning Center Programs:

  Part A – Family Learning Centers: $3,000,000.
  Part B – Library Literacy Centers: $3,000,000.

No funds are authorized for VII unless the total amount appropriated for I, II, and III equals or exceeds the total appropriated for those titles for the preceding fiscal year, plus 4 percent.

Meanwhile, on the funding front, House and Senate Appropriations Committees have begun hearings on the administration's budget proposals for fiscal year 1991 (1 October 1990-30 September 1991). Simultaneously, House and Senate Budget Committees are developing their respective budget resolutions, which ultimately will cut up the fiscal pie to be parceled out to the appropriations subcommittees to further divide among the thousands of competing programs. This is where we have our work cut out for us.

President Bush submitted his budget to Congress on 29 January 1990, recommending a 71.4 percent cut in our categorical library programs: the Library Services and Construction Act (LSCA) and Title II of the Higher Education Act (HEA). That amounts to a drop from fiscal year 1990's appropriation of $136,646,000 to $39,062,000. Having said that, let me stress that the administration's budget is a recommendation. Remember. The president proposes and Congress disposes. According to the Constitution, Congress has the power of the purse. Our job is to convince them that the administration is wrong. We have been fighting proposals to completely eliminate these library programs for the last eight years. What may be confusing to Congress this year is that the administration is recommending a little something for libraries. Of course, it is tempting to cut wherever possible in view of the crushing budget deficit.

The administration budget would cut $101 million by eliminating LSCA I and II–public library services and public library construction. LSCA III, interlibrary cooperation would be increased by 4 percent, going from $19.5 million to $20.3 million, and LSCA VI, library literacy programs, would go up 56 percent, from $5.3 million to $8.3 million. The Higher Education Act Title II library programs would be level funded at last year's level: $844,000 for II-B training and research; $5.7 million for II-C research libraries; and $3.7 million for II-D college library technology.

At a budget briefing, Secretary of Education Lauro Cavazos was asked why LSCA I was zeroed out in view of the fact that it is targeted to his own budget priorities of assistance to the disadvantaged, the illiterate, the handicapped, and minorities. He answered that it was a duplicate program. Charles Kolb, Deputy Undersecretary for the Office of Planning, Budget, and Evaluation, by way of further explanation, added that the program had been around for 35 years and had been very successful. Now, the level of state and local support makes it a lower priority. Department of Education budget documents don't provide any better rationale for the proposed cuts. Regarding LSCA I: "No funds are requested because general assistance is no longer necessary to increase access to library services. Under pending legislation to reauthorize this program, federal dollars are insufficiently focused on those with greatest needs." On LSCA II: "Federal support is no longer necessary, and no funds are requested for this program."

Other programs of the Office of Educational Research and Improvement would be increased from $95,241,000 to $174,728,000–an 83.5 percent increase–to include additional research, data gathering, assessment, plus the education summit followup. Overall, the education budget would be increased only 2 percent from $24.1 billion to $24.6 billion. It seems likely that library programs suffered so that higher departmental priorities could be increased.

Rep. Pat Williams (D-MT), Chairman of the House Postsecondary Education Subcommittee, who has been managing the LSCA bill, issued a statement about the administration's education budget in which he listed support for public libraries as one of the major Bush cuts. Rep. Williams said that, "President Bush should explain to the nation's parents and students how it is that his two-percent increase for the military is a severe cut but his two-percent increase for education is a major increase."

Before the budget was released, two alternate plans were announced on 22 January 1990. House Education and Labor Committee Chairman Augustus Hawkins (D-CA) proposed doubling the education budget to fund proven, successful education programs and restore education to a high national priority. He said the increase could be achieved by reprogramming current budget priorities, without new taxes.

In this twenty-fifth anniversary year of the Elementary and Secondary Education Act and the Higher Education Act, the Committee for Education Funding (CEF) called on Congress and the president to fully fund the programs designed to open doors to the American dream for children and adults. CEF, a coalition of 100 organizations, including ALA, outlined a proposal to double the education budget to a level of $55 billion, including increases of $1.5 billion for programs such as graduate and international education and libraries.

Budget Issues

Before getting on with the rest of the federal legislative agenda, I would like to refer once more to the Congressional Budget Committee process. This came into being in 1974 via the Congressional Budget and Impoundment Control Act, in reaction to President Nixon's outrageous impoundment of hundreds of millions of education and library program dollars in 1973. Once established, the work of the House and Senate Budget Committees has tended to overshadow their counterpart Appropriations Committees and seems, at times, to confuse constituents and to cause some friction with their colleagues on Appropriations. In any event, Budget Committee members are frequently quoted in the news these days as they query administration witnesses, looking for the so-called peace dividend as one country after another turns from communism to democracy. In an election year, a windfall peace dividend appears to be a welcome reprieve from considering a possible call for a tax increase while President Bush continues to say, "Read my lips – No new taxes."[1]

Two tax-related issues are being discussed these days. One is the effort of Sen. Daniel Moynihan (D-NY), Chairman of the Senate Finance Subcommittee on Social Security, to roll back this year's social security payroll tax increase and return social security to a pay-as-you-go basis. His rationale is that the Social Security Trust Funds are now running huge surpluses as planned, but the federal government is not saving these funds. It is spending them, leaving IOUs in their place, and thereby masking the fact that the deficit would otherwise be well over $200 billion rather that the

$123.8 billion stated in the fiscal year 1991 federal government budget document.

The second tax-related issue has to do with the House Ways and Means Committee reviewing the effects of the 1986 Tax Reform Act and such matters as the unrelated business income tax (UBIT), which could have an adverse impact on nonprofit organizations, churches, museums, and libraries. Many business groups, especially small business, have complained that they are at a disadvantage in competing with not-for-profit organizations. No action has been taken so far, but there has been a good deal of behind-the-scenes meeting going on over the past two years. It is expected that the IRS will be issuing a report later this year on its monitoring of tax payments by not-for-profit organizations on UBIT activities.

The Higher Education Act

Anticipating that Congress would begin considering the revision of the Higher Education Act (HEA) this year, the Department of Education held a series of hearings around the country last fall. ALA President-elect Richard Dougherty testifies on behalf of the association in Washington, D.C., highlighting two overriding needs that will affect ALA's recommendations for HEA reauthorization: (1) assistance in taking advantage of the continued and increasing extent to which technology is altering the profile of library service; and (2) aid in combating the increasing shortage of library professionals, particularly Ph.D. faculty members, minorities, and certain specializations. The shortage of faculty members in graduate library schools is severe and growing, a problem with dire consequences for the education of the next generation of librarians and for future research in the field.

Anyone concerned about the possibilities for potential HEA program support in the near future should be thinking now what shape we want to see this legislation take. We need facts and figures to help justify whatever case we make to Congress.

The National Literacy Act of 1990

The National Literacy Act of 1990 (S. 1310), introduced by Sen. Paul Simon (D-IL) with 35 cosponsors, passed the Senate on 6 February 1990 by a unanimous vote. (It helps to have a First Lady in the White House who has made literacy her cause.) The bill would establish or expand a number of literacy programs. For example, Title IV, Books for Families, would amend Title VI of LSCA to give priority to programs and services that "(1) will be delivered in areas of greatest need which have highest concentrations of adults who do not have a secondary education or its equivalent, and which

(A) have few community or financial resources to establish the program described under this section without Federal assistance or (B) have low per capita income, unemployment or underemployment, and (2) coordinate with literacy organizations and community based organizations providing literacy services."

A new program of model library literacy centers would be authorized under LSCA VI, with grants up to $200,000 and an authorization of $2 million. Those who would like to see more detail regarding this Senate-passed literacy bill can check it out in the 6 February 1990 *Congressional Record*, pp. S 825-32. The House companion bill (HR 3123) will be marked up by the House Education and Labor Committee.

Information Access Issues

In the broad category of information access, are a number of developing issues, both regulatory and legislative, which have been around for a while and will, no doubt, continue in importance well beyond the 1991 White House Conference. We will discuss several topics in the following pages.

The issue of telecommunications access charges and their impact on libraries as they would be passed through from value-added networks is quite important. ALA filed comments in August 1989 in the Federal Communications Commission CC Docket 89-79 relating to the creation of access charge subelements for open network architecture.

The proposed National Research and Education Network (NREN) legislation was reintroduced by Sen. Albert Gore (D-TN) in 1989 (S 1067) and has been redrafted. Meanwhile, the president's science advisor, D. Allan Bromley, director of the Science and Technology Policy, issued the Federal High Performance Computing Program, which is a very similar plan. The administration's view, however, is that no legislation is necessary and that they would prefer to proceed through administration action. The NREN would upgrade and expand the existing interconnected array of mostly scientific research networks such as the national NSFNET and ARPANET and the regional networks such as NYSERNET and SURANET, known collectively as the internet.

The Paperwork Reduction Act (PRA) was first established in 1980 during the Carter administration to reduce the paperwork and regulatory burden on business and others. PRA expired 20 September 1989, while the provisions of the controversial draft bills were still being analyzed and debated. During the Reagan Administration, the Office of Management and Budget (OMB) had interpreted PRA to include authority over government information dissemination in ways that have reduced and privatized dissemination of government information. The prime example is OMB

Circular A-130, their controversial policy directive dealing with the management of federal information resources.

Subsequently, reauthorization bills, S. 1742 and HR 3695, were introduced by Sen. Jeff Bingaman (D-NM), Chairman of the Government Information and Regulation Subcommittee, and Rep. John Conyers (D-MI), Chairman of the Government Operations Committee. Proponents of the bills claim that OMB's power over government information dissemination policy will be defined and therefore limited. Librarians see OMB as being given clear authority to second guess an agency's decisions about how to fulfill its information dissemination functions. OMB guidance would require government agencies, before disseminating information products and services, to consider a list of six factors. Particularly vexing is the fourth of these six factors: "If an information product or service is equivalent to an agency product or service and reasonably achieves the dissemination objectives of the agency product or service." Lawyers could put their children through school deciding what's equivalent and what's reasonable.

Reinforcing ALA's concern about giving OMB excessive power over agencies is the Supreme Court's 7 to 2 decision handed down 21 February 1990 in the case of Dole v. United Steelworkers of America. The Court ruled that OMB can no longer block regulations requiring companies to provide health, safety, and other consumer information to workers or the public on the grounds that the disclosures require excessive paperwork.

On 12 March 1990, four Republican Senators—Rudman (NH), Roth (DE), Stevens (AK), and Boschwitz (MN)—introduced S. 2261, a four-year simple extension bill. Their rationale was that there were still too many questions about PRA that needed to be answered. They needed more time to consider the implications of the 65-page Senate bill, S. 1742.

On 13 March 1990, the House Government Operations Committee ordered their version of the PRA, HR 3695, reported out of committee. The Senate Governmental Affairs Committee was not scheduled to "mark up" their bill until 29 March.

The Government Printing Office Improvement Act of 1990, HR 3849, is closely related to PRA with its potentially negative impact on the Depository Library Program. HR 3849 would change the definition of *government publication* in Title 44 of the *U.S. Code* to exclude electronic information services such as bulletin boards and other online data. For the first time in the history of the Depository Library Program, users would have to pay for access to government information. As introduced, this bill would dismantle the only available avenue of "no fee" access to all electronic forms of government information.

Hearings were held 7 and 8 March 1990 before the House Administration Procurement and Printing Subcommittee, chaired by Rep. Jim Bates (D-CA). ALA's witness was Katherine F. Maudsley, associate university librarian for public services, University of California at Davis. She spoke against restricting the definition of *government publication* to products only. She pointed out that, contrary to the bill's reference to *cost sharing*, the proposal amounts to cost shifting, which would reduce federal expenditures by increasing even further the expenses already borne by the institutions and state and local governments that support depository libraries. Information appended to her testimony shows that the most active 6 percent of depository libraries spend at least $21.4 million annually to provide public access to government information. That is more than the Government Printing Office fiscal year 1990 appropriation to distribute the information to all of the nearly 1,400 depositories.

S.J. Res. 57, introduced by Sen. Claiborne Pell (D-RI) to establish a national policy to promote and encourage the printing of books and other publications of enduring value on alkaline paper, was passed by the Senate on 31 July 1989. The House companion bill, H.J. Res. 226, introduced by Rep. Pat Williams (D-MT), is pending with some 70 cosponsers. On 21 February the Subcommittee on Government Information, Justice and Agriculture of the House Government Operations Committee held a hearing on the measure with statements of support from the librarian of Congress, the U.S. archivist, and the chairman of the Association of American Publishers. At an earlier appropriations hearing, the U.S. public printer indicated GPO support for H.J. Res. 226. To get the bill out of the Government Operations Committee, which has been concentrating its attention on the PRA legislation, at least 218 cosponsors are needed.

The Bush administration is requesting $372,592,000 in fiscal year 1991 for postal revenue forgone (appropriation to compensate the postal service for rates that are lower than full costs such as the library rate and the not-for-profit rate). That's 23 percent, or $112 million, less than the U.S. Postal Service estimates is needed for the subsidy to keep at current levels the preferred postal rates used by schools, colleges, libraries, and nonprofit groups. Budget documents explain that the difference is due to proposals (suggested by the Postal Rate Commission and others over the past few years) to restrict the use of some rates.

Preferred rate status would be terminated or restricted for the following categories: (a) second-class nonprofit mail whose content includes more than 10 percent advertising; (b) third-class nonprofit mail with advertising that does not relate directly to the primary purpose of the organization or that includes political advocacy, and educational material for organizations that are not schools; and (c) fourth-class library rates for publishers' mailings to libraries or schools.

The fourth-class library rate is now 87 cents for a two-pound package. The unsubsidized rate is 92 cents–a 6 percent increase–without considering the rate increase proposed by the Postal Service for 1991. If this recommendation were approved by Congress, libraries that receive publishers' shipments via the mail could expect to have this increase to publishers passed on to the, and we all know every dollar spent on postage is a dollar less spent on books and other library resources.

Except for the postal subsidy, the preceding half-dozen items, which I have called information access issues, reflect how we spend an increasing amount of time in the ALA Washington office on legislative and regulatory matters that do not result in any direct financial aid to libraries. It is important to put these in perspective and consider the time and effort to be an investment in the future of librarianship and in our ability to provide and facilitate improved and up-to-date library and information services for our diverse population.

Conclusion

By way of summary, I was sorely tempted to add to my bibliography the 1,269-page *Budget of the United States Government, Fiscal Year 1991*, which sells for $38.00 from GPO. On second thought, I suggest a much better buy, if you don't already have access to it – a subscription to the *ALA Washington Newsletter*, which costs $25 and covers the various items I have mentioned provides congressional committee lists and reprints from the *Congressional Record* and *Federal Register* when appropriate.

Finally, now is the time to rally the troops to urge Congress to reject the administration's proposal to zero out LSCA I and II and to provide at least $85 million for Public Library Services – last year's level ($82.5 million) plus a 4 percent for inflation – and $25 million for Public Library Construction – less than half of the $55 million authorized in the new LSCA and the $50 million appropriated way back in fiscal year 1983.

The White House Conference on Library and Information Services will be held 9-13 July 1991. Another $1,025,000 is needed to complete full funding of the $6 million authorized to help carry out the second WHCLIS. Illinois lead the parade of state level activities with their Governor's Conference.

This process is an opportunity to gain widespread attention and build public awareness of the critical issues in your state for your libraries and services of all types. If we believe that information is the currency of democracy, then as librarians we must continually remind ourselves, as well as others, that libraries are dealing with the coin of the realm.

Note

1. The president changed his no-tax position in September 1990.

State Legislation: Current and Developing

BRIDGET L. LAMONT

Director
Illinois State Library
Springfield, Illinois

If one believes the adage, "Good government is good politics," then libraries should be well positioned for positive consideration by politicians at the local and state levels. The theme of democracy, specifically libraries and information services for democracy, is included as a major theme of the 1991 White House Conference on Library and Information Services. Although the search for this term was elusive in the early deliberations of the NCLIS White House Conference Preliminary Design Group, committee members shared an enthusiastic commitment and keen perspective on the importance of libraries and information in the democratic process.

As the Preliminary Design Group noted, "Information is a crucial resource in a democratic society. . .Government decision making is not the sole responsibility of elected or paid officials; a democratic society depends upon the informed participation of its people." Libraries and democracy. How do we most effectively convey this responsibility to librarians? How will we be most successful in, on one hand, putting libraries on the pedestal with democracy as good and right and, on the other, ensuring a place for libraries on the list of survival services necessary to function today and even more so in the twenty-first century? Or should we adopt the motto used by Citicorp, "When you don't want to just *survive* but *succeed*"? Libraries and success?

As lobbyists (and we are, regardless of title or institutional affiliation, *if* we believe in our product), librarians are in an enviable position. We are in a period where service industries are growing quickly and emerging as major forces in the work place, economy, and society. Libraries are known for making the most out of their money and responding to community needs with tight budgeting, long-range planning, and creative use of available resources (perhaps too creative). As the Illinois Secretary of State Jim Edgar often says, he "knows of no group that does so much with limited tax dollars." In terms of marketing, librarians have a positive quality of life product. People feel *good* about libraries.

My experience with legislators indicates that legislators like to do things that will impact the local community–equate that to mean the individual voter–and many have nostalgic feelings about a favorite book or the librarian who helped them when they attended fifth grade. In fact, legislators have been characterized as tolerant and benevolent about libraries, viewing libraries as all-American. Are these perceptions about libraries too comfortable for the challenges libraries must meet in this information era?

A review of the services provided by the 101 companies in *The Service Edge*[1] does not list a single library, although the book's premise is that good service is important to Americans and there are companies able to provide high-quality service delivery. In his introduction to the book, Tom Peters writes, ". . . superb service is becoming a requirement for survival in our fragmenting, fast changing, quality conscious and ever more competitive markets. 'Service added'–unheard-of responsiveness, 'smarter' products, and consultative service add-ons–are redefining almost every industry."[2] There is no doubt in my mind that libraries have or should or must fit it. We have the product and we have the commitment. This issue remains one of education and promotion–just how do books, serials, and online information services make a difference?

Much of the work resides in the state-based legislative work handled by state libraries, state library associations, and grass roots advocates for libraries. In preparation for my essay, I am grateful to my colleagues, the state librarians, who responded to my request for information on state legislative efforts.

In my request for information from state librarians for this essay, these four questions were asked: (1) What has been the most significant legislative effort in your state in the last two years? (2) What is the primary library legislation identified or issues determined? (3) How is library legislation identified or issues determined? (4) Are there other current legislative issues in your state that may affect libraries?

Robert Clark, state librarian of Oklahoma, notes, "A public policy issue must have a crisis setting, must be controversial and must be clearly understood by the public whose lives it affects."[3] So just where do libraries fit into the picture? How do the enormous energy, exhausting and intensive time given to the development of library legislation platforms, use of legislative networks, and workshops on library legislation relate to today's public policy issues? State governments face issues of mental health, drugs, environment, prisons, and so on. After looking at the range of issues, they may find library legislative issues to be a respite in the action, which may not always be to our advantage.

An article on Florida's "sunrise" legislation notes, "Legislatures face a problem of being bombarded with demands for action on minor issues."[4] The same may be said for library legislative platforms, which may take a scattershot approach to legislation – that is, they may tackle any issues affecting libraries – or they may be so philosophical that they dilute the issues. Trying to do something for everyone is a criticism sometimes made of libraries. The Florida legislative approach merits attention because it is a strategic planning effort initiated at the legislative level to filter issues for legislative attention. The working group also included dozens of outsiders. The Florida story includes this assessment: "Legislators had better plan well into the next century and defy *immediate political pressures* (quick-fix solutions for libraries) if they hope to assure their state's survival in the tough new international economy."

By the same token, librarians had best plan well into the future. They must provide studies and data to support their legislative initiative, speak with authority on the essentiality of libraries for ensuring informed decisions, and show the library's impact at the local level on the community's quality of life. In Illinois, we take heart in the comment made by an official of our state's Department of Commerce and Community Affairs who noted she has not taken a single company considering locating in Illinois on a community tour where questions were not asked about the local library! This certainly supports the premise in our recent study of the role of local public libraries in economic development efforts, arguing the public library's role in nurturing small business development and providing information resources to governing officials.

In presenting legislative initiatives, state librarians identified these concerns related to funding: public education finance, overreliance on property tax, property tax freeze, revision of tax structure, and restructuring of public education. Local public libraries and funding for those libraries are clearly the priority legislative concern in the states' library legislative platforms for 1990. There are legislative proposals in many states for increased state aid for public libraries along with a broader concern about issues relating to property taxes and libraries. State librarians referred to needs for *basic funding* for public libraries, maintenance of state aid monies, and increasing state aid. Parenthetically, the priority attention given to public libraries is somewhat surprising to me in these times when multitype library collaboration and growth of networks are a given. This may relate to the statutory scope of a state library agency's responsibility by type of library or respond to what I believe is a legislator's propensity for helping local, that is, community public libraries. It most likely reflects how very far we will need to go in terms of state support for libraries, particularly funding. Regrettably, this attitude supports the U.S. Department of Education's reluctance to flip-flop LSCA Title I (local library services) and Title III (multitype library cooperation) monies. One has to be impressed, though, with the very confident replies and successful legislative initiatives undertaken in the states where pride is measured not so much by the actual appropriation, but by percentage increases or even by the basic *establishment* of state aid for public libraries.

Education reform is the issue today, and the momentum has been building over the last three years. The potential for libraries will be enormous if we make our case that libraries, cooperating with community colleges, are part of the educational process, especially in the areas of adult education and literacy. Librarians should understand the impact of aid to education when developing strategies for library funding. While we have made strides in positioning libraries as part of the education platform, we need to be prepared to comment *now* on the threats of property tax reform and its implications for funding for education, libraries, and other local government services. I believe we are in a vulnerable position with the public library and, in some states, with community college library funding. We are caught, because of our reliance on property taxes for public library monies, without adequate national discussion or a major study of alternative methods for funding libraries. (Ohio has traditionally been the exception to the rule.)

While the National Commission on Libraries and Information Science or the American Library Association's Public Library Association should take the lead in a study of alternatives to the property tax for funding libraries, we need the insight of nonlibrarians such as the state and local government budget officials, taxpayers' groups, economic and fiscal specialists, and others.

Montana reported a notable string of successes, including the establishment of a per capita and per square mile funding for public library federations, a statewide library card, interlibrary loan reimbursement, and base grants for public library federations. Interestingly, funds for interlibrary loan reimbursement were nearly four times greater than grants for the public library federations. (One can interpret this as a positive statement on interlibrary cooperation although payment for resource sharing is alarming to me with my strong bias against reimbursement for cooperating. Three other states reported on legislative successes with net lender reimbursement or statewide access such as Iowa's Open Access Program.)

With these issues, there is impetus for another study on the scope of interlibrary loan reimbursement in the states and the message being sent on interlibrary cooperation, resource sharing, and local library responsibilities. Will these data support the librarian who needs to answer a board or faculty when it wants to know why materials are loaned to other libraries? Or will it backfire and be used to fan the eternal flame in the hearts of some librarians who continue to anguish over the inequities of life or, in this case, the fact that some libraries have more to share and some libraries do share more?

Some creative legislative proposals have been reported that merit tracking by the other states and the American Library Association. Here are some I would like to hear more about: what public libraries may or may not charge for, performance as a criterion for aid for public libraries, requirements for all school *buildings* to have a certified school librarian, and community college automation centers. Some of the areas addressed in the responses to my survey were a cultural services initiative act and its relationship to the state library agency, redesign of a library network, volunteer protection act, personnel in public libraries, control of the library for the blind and physically handicapped, establishment of a state literacy office in a state library, recodification of district library laws, and requirement to use acid-free paper in state publications. Notably, only one state responding to my survey referred to the state's pre-White House Conference on Library and Information Services and that was to report a successful appropriation of funds from the state legislature to fund state pre-White House Conference activities.

While funding is the priority, it is also important to note that states continue to deal with legislation on confidentiality, library theft, and censorship. This seems to be anticipatory rather than responsive state legislation – happily.

I was also curious about how library legislation is developed and found, as one state librarian noted, "Everyone has a hand in identifying issues." This is not a surprise because librarians are one of the *most* democratic groups – just look at the ALA process! By everyone, librarians meant the state library agency, state library associations, librarians, legislative staff, legislators, governors, and friends of library groups. Six of the states responding indicated the involvement of a lobbyist paid by the state library association, and, in some states, the state librarian is actually registered as a lobbyist. I particularly enjoyed the comment by the state librarian who indicated that the association's legislative committee develops a long and *unpriced* statement of needs. Remember what I suggested about a scattershot and unrealistic approach? It is easy to ask – and appropriate to make your needs known – but who takes the responsibility for making the hard decisions in library funding priorities?

I have been very intrigued by an article from the *Kettering Review* called "The Misery of Politics and the Sphere of Government," which discusses how in "classical republican tradition, the life of politics was held up as an ideal." However, the author compares that position to the one taken by our founding fathers who "themselves experienced politics as unpleasant, intrusive and undignified."[5]

It is time for librarians to decide if they will take the classical tradition or the position of our founders as experienced in this article. Good government is good politics, and providing timely and responsive services should translate into political successes for more libraries. We have three hard decisions to make–personally and professionally–about legislative action (while we can rejoice at many consistent small victories, we must try new or expanded tactics):

1. To what extent will we financially support a candidate?

2. How can libraries continue to be nonpartisan while librarians learn to make bipartisan contacts on behalf of library issues?

3. When will we learn to be savvy and tie our issues into state and national legislative priorities or public policy concerns?

As Joe Shubert, New York State librarian, in response to my survey, wrote: "I believe that each of the major increases in general operating support for systems (New York) . . . was substantially driven by programs that legislators embraced as relating to state priorities. I think we saw some of the same things in the LSCA reauthorization. Congressmen support our continuing programs and want to put something extra in, and we have to find a way of negotiating through the different perspectives."

We must lobby as librarians for our services and our products, but we must think like politicians to promote libraries and enjoy legislative successes just as legislators select issues that appeal to groups of constituents. We are a service industry, and we are in the information business, whether it be bestsellers or Fortune 500 corporate information needs. *Information Anxiety* is not only the name of a book but a fact with which we need to deal to make hard decisions. The book suggests, "Not only are we overwhelmed by the sheer amount of information, most of us are also hampered by an education that inadequately trains us to process it."[6] This is not a library science textbook so, in this case, do not include yourself in the *us* – include yourself as part of the solution.

The array of library legislation pending in the states reflects the diversity of the states and responsiveness to local needs. A number of proposals merit tracking, however, so others can consider adapting programs. Clearly there is an ambitious library legislative agenda in the states.

We are not out of shots, but we would best be clear what we are using to gain legislative attention and priority consideration for libraries. We must capitalize on the positive impressions of libraries and position libraries as part of the successful resolution of the many difficult public policy issues today.

Notes

1. Ron Zemke with Dick Schaaf, *The Service Edge: 101 Companies That Profit from Customer Care* (New York: New American Library, 1989).

2. Ibid., xi-xviii.

3. Robert C. Clark, Jr., "Legislative Support of Library Services in Oklahoma," in *Libraries in the Political Process*, ed. E.J. Josey (Phoenix: Oryx Press, 1980), 123-29.

4. Neal R. Peirce, "Florida's Sunrise–Can a Legislature Look Forward?" *Nations, Cities Weekly*, 26 January 1987.

5. John Patrick Diggins, "The Misery of Politics and the Sphere of Government," *Kettering Review*, Fall 1988, 6-7.

6. Richard Saul Wurman, *Information Anxiety* (New York: Doubleday, 1989).

Appendix
Basic Guidelines for Disaster Planning

TOBY MURRAY

Illinois State Library Preservation Office
Springfield, Illinois

Disasters can happen to all of us – in libraries large and small. Knowing what (and what *not*) to do before, during, and after a disaster will prevent panic, lessen damage, and enable library staffs to implement an organized recovery. The following guidelines are offered to assist you in the preparation of a disaster plan and the organization of salvage procedures for your own institution. They should be tailored to fit your institution's needs and idiosyncrasies. Members of your library's disaster planning committee should receive two copies of the plan – one to keep at work and one to keep at home. The plan should be reviewed and updated at least twice a year.

Disaster Prevention

Man-made disasters can often be prevented by routine inspections of a facility. Temperature and humidity, ideally, should be maintained at a constant 68 degrees and 50 percent relative humidity. Cleaning and spraying for insects and rodents should be performed on a regular basis. Materials should be properly stored and protected from dirt, dust, and light. Ultraviolet filters should be placed over fluorescent lights and on windows. Leaky pipes, frayed electrical wires, untended machinery, open windows, and structural

143

damage can result in unnecessary destruction of materials and possible loss of life. Aisles and work areas should be kept free of unprocessed materials and trash.

Machinery should be unplugged when not in use. Rules regarding food, beverages, smoking, and unauthorized access should be established and enforced. Security checks should be made at closing time to ensure that all exits and windows are locked, all equipment has been turned off, no cigarettes are smoldering in ashtrays or wastebaskets, and no unauthorized persons are in the building.

Disasters do not appear out of nowhere. Be aware of all hazards (situations that have potential for causing damage) and correct them before they develop into disasters. Staff members should all be familiar with the layout of the building and of possible danger areas. They should know the location of all fire extinguishers and alarms, and they should know how to operate them. Fire exits and alternate escape routes should be clearly marked. Evacuation procedures should be established and practiced regularly.

All sources of supplies should be contacted in advance to explain your needs and purpose. Sources should be contacted on a regular basis to determine whether those supplies and services are still available and to remind them of their commitment. Keep in mind that in a wide-scale, major disaster, your sources may not be available because they have their own damages with which to deal or because they are assisting someone else. In addition, outside help probably will not be available for one or two weeks. It is recommended that you keep as many recovery materials as possible onsite.

DISASTER PLAN FORM

I.   **Name of institution**_____

II.   **Date of completion or update of this form**_____

III.   **Staff members to be called in the event of a disaster:**

Position	Name	Telephone Numbers Home Office
Chief library administrator	_____	
Person in charge of building maintenance	_____	
In-house disaster recovery team members	_____	
	_____	
	_____	
	_____	
	_____	
	_____	

Note below who is to call whom upon the discovery of a disaster ("telephone tree").

IV.   **Off-site services to be called (if needed) in the event of a disaster.**

Service	Name	Telephone Numbers Home Office
Fire dept.		
Police dept.		
Ambulance		
Illinois ESDA		
Insurance co.		
Legal advisor		
Utility companies		
Electrician		
Plumber		
Carpenter		
Exterminator		
Chemist		
Mycologist		
Locksmith		
Janitorial service		

Individuals
and/or
organizations
to assist in
clean-up

_____

_____

_____

_____

_____

Illinois State   Cheryl Pence (217) 524-5866
Library
Preservation
Office

V.   **Upkeep checklist**

A. Daily procedures

Locks on doors and windows secure and all keys accounted

for

No pipes, faucets, toilets, or air-conditioning units leaking

Electrical equipment unplugged; no frayed wiring in

evidence

No signs of structural damage

No burning materials in ashtrays and wastebaskets

B. Periodic procedures   Date Checked

Emergency numbers posted by each
phone
                                               _____

Most recent inspection by fire
department
                                               _____

     Fire extinguishers operable   _____

     Smoke alarms operable   _____

     Sprinkler system operable   _____

     Water detectors operable   _____

Public address system operable   _____

Operable flashlights placed
in every department
                                               _____

Transistor radio operable   _____

Staff familiarized (by tour, not map) with
locations of fire extinguishers, flashlights,
radio, storm shelter, and how to reach
members of the in-house disaster recovery
team
                                               _____

Most recent fire drill   _____

Most recent civil defense drill   _____

Most recent tornado drill   _____

Most recent inventory (see IX below)   _____

Current insurance policy (attach a copy)   _____

Completed copy of "Fire and Insurance
Protection of Library Resources"
Questionnaire from *Protecting the
Library and Its Resources*, Chicago: ALA,
1963 (attach a copy)   _____

VI.   **Locations of in-house emergency equipment (attach map
       or floor plan with locations marked and labeled)**

       Cut-off switches and valves   <u>Location</u>

              Electric   _____

              Gas   _____

              Water   _____

              Sprinkler system
              (if separate)   _____

              Disaster supply
                kit   _____

       Extension cords,
       heavy-duty   _____

       Fans   _____

       Fire alarms   _____

       Fire extinguishers   _____

       First aid kits   _____

       Flashlights   _____

       Freezer paper   _____

       Mops   _____

       Nylon monofilament
       (fishing line)   _____

       Paper towel   _____

Plastic sheeting _____

Plastic trash
 bags _____

Rubber gloves _____

Smoke alarms _____

Sponges, pails,
 brooms _____

Transistor radio _____

Unprinted
 newsprint _____

Water detectors _____

Water hoses _____

Wet-dry vacuum _____

Date members of in-house
disaster recovery team
 toured all locations
 noted above _____

VII.   **Sources of off-site equipment and supplies**

Item	Contact	Telephone Number
CB radio		
Dehumidifiers		
Drying space		
Fans		
Forklift		
Freezer facilities		
Fungicides		
Freezer paper		
Generator, portable		
Hard hats		

Library trucks _____

Pallets _____

Paper towel _____

Plastic milk crates _____

Plastic sheeting _____

Refrigerator trucks _____

Security staff, extra _____

Sump pump,
 portable _____

Temperature
humidity gauges _____

Unprinted
 newsprint _____

Waterproof
 clothing _____

Wet-dry vacuums _____

VIII.   **All locations where this plan and follow-up reports are on file**

                    Date Filed
A. In-house   _____

                _____

                _____

                _____

                _____

B. Off-site

    _____

    _____

    _____

    _____

    _____

C. Please send a copy to the Illinois State Library Preservation Office, 288 Centennial Building, Springfield, IL 62756.

IX.   **Inventory/priority lists**

Attach, *for each department,* a priority list for salvage should a disaster occur. To simplify this procedure, assign priorities as follows:

#1 – Salvage at all costs.

#2 – Salvage if time permits.

#3 – Salvage as part of general clean-up.

The following questions may be helpful in determining priorities:

A.   Can the item be replaced? At what cost?

B.   Would the cost of replacement be more or less than restoration of the item?

C.   How important is the item to the collection?

D.   Is the item available elsewhere?

Perhaps the highest priority should be given to bibliographic controls of your collection, such as card catalogs, shelf lists, inventories, and finding aids. It is strongly recommended that duplicate copies of these controls be kept off-site.

Special collections will most likely be second on your priority list. Staff should know, for example, that unique local history materials should be salvaged before the *National Geographics*.

X.   **Procedures**

Attach a list of specific procedures to be followed in the event of a disaster in your library, including responsibilities of in-house disaster recovery team members and work crews. See "Salvage Procedures for Water-Damaged Materials," which follows.

DISASTER RECOVERY

If a disaster strikes when the building is occupied, your first concern should be for the safety of the individuals inside. Escape routes, alternate routes, and procedures for evacuating the building should be clear to all personnel and visitors. Practice drills should be conducted on a regular basis to eliminate panic during the real thing.

Most disasters tend to occur when the building is unoccupied – during the early morning hours, on weekends, or during holiday closings. In the event of a major disaster, do not enter the building until it has been declared safe to do so by emergency personnel.

Ninety-five percent of all disasters will result in water-damaged materials. **Keep in mind that mold will form within 48 to 72 hours in a warm, humid environment. You must work quickly to salvage damaged materials and to prevent additional damage from occurring.**

The following steps are recommended for an effective recovery operation:

I.   **Assess the damage.**

How much damage has occurred? What kind of damage is it? (fire, smoke, soot, clean water, dirty water?) Is it confined to one area or is the entire building damaged? How much of the collection has been affected? What types of materials have been damaged? Are the damaged items easily replaced, or are they irreplaceable? Can they be salvaged by the in-house recovery team, or will outside help be required?

II.   **Stabilize the environment.**

The environment must be stabilized to prevent the growth of mold. Ideal conditions for a recovery operation are 65 degrees Fahrenheit and 50 percent relative humidity.

The following equipment should be readily accessible to help stabilize the environment.

A. Portable generators, in case a power failure occurs

B. Pumps, to remove large quantities of standing water

C. Fans, to circulate the air

D. Thermometers, hygrometers, hygrothermographs, and/or sling psychrometers, to measure the temperature and humidity

Dehumidifiers can help to lower the humidity, but they usually are effective only in small, enclosed areas and tend to increase the temperature in a room. They can also freeze up in the lower temperatures required for salvage and recovery operations. **Raising the temperature will not lower the humidity–it will only accelerate mold growth.** Temperature and humidity should be monitored constantly.

Air should be circulated in the damaged area. This may be accomplished by running fans constantly. If possible, they should expel the humid air from the area. Any standing water should be pumped from the area. Extreme caution must be taken, as standing water can conceal hazards.

III.   **Activate the in-house disaster recovery team.**

Organize work crews and be sure their responsibilities are clearly defined. No salvage activity should begin until a plan of action has been determined by the team leader. Disaster and recovery areas should be inaccessible to the public.

Frequent rest breaks should be provided for workers. Food and beverages should be available.

IV.   **Restore the area.**

After the damaged items have been removed and the environment has been stabilized, the area must be thoroughly cleaned. Walls, floors, ceilings, and all furniture and equipment must be scrubbed with soap and water and a fungicide. Carpeting, especially the padding under it, should be carefully examined, as mold will develop rapidly. Removal of smoke odor and fogging with fungicides and insecticides should be performed only by professionals.

SALVAGE PROCEDURES FOR WATER-DAMAGED MATERIALS

A number of options are available for treating water-damaged materials. The choice of treatment will depend on the extent and type of damage incurred and the manpower, expertise, and facilities available.

I.   **Freezing**

Freezing wet materials will stabilize them and provide you with time to determine your course of action. Mold will not grow and further deterioration from water will not occur when materials are in a frozen state. Books have been left in a freezer for ten years and then successfully thawed and air dried with no resulting damage. Freezing will also help to eliminate smoke odor from materials.

Rapid freezing is recommended to minimize damage from ice crystals (the faster the materials are frozen, the smaller the ice crystals will be). Temperatures below 15 degrees Fahrenheit will freeze and dry out wet materials. If freezer space is not immediately available, and the outside temperature is below 15 degrees Fahrenheit, place the materials in a secure area outside. Cover them with plastic if rain or snow is expected.

Freezing is an intermediate stage. After materials have been removed from the freezer, they must be placed in a vacuum freeze dryer or air dried.

II.   **Vacuum freeze drying**

Vacuum freeze drying is the safest and most successful method, although it is also the most expensive. Materials **must** be already frozen when they are placed in a sublimation chamber. This type of chamber operates under high vacuum and high heat and turns the ice crystals inside and on the frozen materials to water vapor. The vapor is then collected on a cold panel that has been chilled to at least 200 degrees F, so it cannot go back on the materials. If they are not frozen when they are put in the chamber, the materials will freeze on the outside and the water molecules on the inside will be forced through the frozen barrier as the vacuum is pulled. This action can cause the book or document to "explode."

When the materials are removed from the vacuum freeze chamber, they will be very dry and should acclimate for a least one month before they are opened to avoid cracking the spine and/or binding (this is especially true for leather bindings). They may be placed in a high humidity room to accelerate the acclimation process, but must be monitored closely for signs of mold.

Materials so treated will not look like new but will show signs of swelling and distortion. Stanford University Library staff members reported that they needed an additional 12 percent of shelf space for materials that had been treated in Lockheed's chamber. Photographs will not be damaged by this treatment, but rubber cement will dissolve and stain the pages to which it has been applied.

III.   **Air drying**

Air drying should be performed only in a stable environment to inhibit the growth of mold. The ideal environment for air drying is 50-60 degrees F and 25-35 percent relative humidity. Instructions are outlined in II below. This process is **not recommended** for coated stock materials such as art books (see III below).

IV.   **Vacuum drying**

Vacuum drying involves the placement of wet materials in a chamber that pulls the moisture by means of a vacuum. This method is **not recommended** as the heat involved is damaging to paper (especially bound paper) and photographic materials. Microwave ovens should not be used for the same reason.

The following salvage procedures are recommended:

I.   **Volumes to be frozen**

A.   Removal

1.   Clear the floors and aisles first.

2.   Begin with the wettest materials. These will usually be on the lowest shelves, unless the water has come in through the ceiling.

3.   Dirt and mold should be removed and treated before freezing (see II.A and VI below). If time does not permit these activities, dirty and/or moldy books may be frozen (mud will easily brush off when it is dry). Silt should be washed out immediately, as it is almost impossible to remove when it is dry.

4.   Pack materials on site, if possible. If it is not possible, remove by human chain.

5. Keep accurate records of the locations from which materials are removed.

B. Packing

1. Remove volumes from shelves in order.

2. Wrap freezer paper around each volume (waxed side next to the volume) and place in plastic crates **spine down.**

3. Pack crates one layer only snugly enough so that volumes will not slide or lean.

4. Wrap open books as found and place on top of a packed container. Do not place more than one open volume in a container. Be sure there is a freezer paper barrier between the packed volumes and the open volume to prevent staining from binding dyes.

5. If books are stuck together, do not attempt to separate them, but pack them as one volume.

6. Pack them in the condition in which they were found. **Do not attempt to close open volumes or open closed volumes that are wet.**

C. Record keeping

1. Label each container with your institution's name and assign it a number.

2. On a separate sheet of paper, record the box number, call numbers of the first and last volumes packed, and the total number of books in each container. If they are not in call number order, note the location where found.

3.   If the containers are sent to more than one freezer, note which container numbers are sent where.

D.   Transporting

1.   Materials should be placed in a freezer facility as quickly as possible to prevent the growth of mold. Care should be taken that containers do not fall over during transport, as further damage may result.

2.   Materials should be placed in refrigerated trucks if they cannot be frozen within 48 hours.

II.   **Volumes to be air dried.**

A.   Washing procedures (to be performed off site only)

1.   Keep the book tightly closed and hold it under cold, clean, running water.

2.   Remove as much mud as possible from the binding by dabbing gently with a sponge. **Do not rub** or use brushes and **do not sponge** the pages or edges, as these actions can force the mud into the spine or the wet pages, causing further damage to the volume. Let the motion of the running water clean off the dirt.

3.   Squeeze the book gently and with even pressure to remove excess water and to reshape the binding.

4.   **Do not wash:**

   a.   Open or swollen volumes.
   b.   Vellum or parchment bindings or pages.
   c.   Full or partial leather bindings.
   d.   Fragile or brittle materials.
   e.   Works of art on paper.
   f.   Water-soluble components (inks, tempera, watercolors, dyes, charcoal, and the like).
   g.   Manuscripts.
   h.   Nonpaper materials.

B.   Saturated volumes

   1.   **Do not open!** Wet paper tears easily!

   2.   Set volumes on their heads on absorbent paper. Pages tend to droop within the binding when a volume is shelved upright, so setting it on its head will counteract this tendency. Plastic sheeting should be placed under the paper toweling or unprinted newsprint to protect tabletops. Turn the volumes right side up when changing the paper beneath them. Their position should be reversed each time the paper is changed and the wet paper removed from the area.

   3.   Covers may be opened to support the volume.

   4.   Aluminum foil may be placed between the cover and the endleaf to prevent staining from the binding dye.

   5.   When most of the water has drained, proceed as for "Damp volumes."

C. Damp volumes

    1. Very carefully open the book (not more than a 30-degree angle).

    2. Begin interleaving from the back and keep the volume in an upright position.

    3. Place interleaving sheets at intervals of 25 leaves (50 pages) unless they will distort the volume.

    4. Change interleaving frequently. Do not reuse unless the sheets are being impregnated with fungicide. Ontho-PhenylPhenl (O-PP) has been found to be less toxic than thymol and is recommended. Mix one pound of O-PP to one gallon of acetone or ethanol (do not use methanol, as it will cause inks to bleed). Safety equipment (mask, eye goggles, and rubber gloves) should be worn when preparing and using this solution.

    5. Continue to change the paper underneath and remove from the area.

D. Slightly damp volumes/volumes with only wet edges

    1. Stand volume on its head and fan open slightly. Paperback books may support each other with a barrier between them or they may be wedged with Styrofoam pieces. Position volumes in the path of circulating air.

    2. When almost dry, lay the volumes flat and place weights (not other drying books) on them to minimize distortion. **Do not stack wet volumes.**

3. Lightweight volumes (less than six pounds) may be hung on lines to dry.

    a. Use monofilament nylon line, not more than 1/32 inches in diameter, not more than five or six feet long, spaced approximately one-half inch apart.
    b. Do not line-dry a saturated volume as the monofilament will cut through the wet paper.

III.   Volumes with coated stock paper

Wet coated stock paper should be handled with care, as the print will slide off the wet page if it is rubbed. **Do not allow wet books with coated stock paper to dry in a closed state as the pages will permanently bond together.** Almost all attempts to separate stuck pages by rewetting them have failed. McDonnell Douglas's Document Reclamation Service reports that vacuum freeze drying of coated stock volumes is rarely successful. Keep volumes submerged until the pages can be separated (see IV.B below). **The only chance of saving such materials is to interleave every page and air dry.**

IV.   Documents/unbound materials

A. Freeze as found

    1. Do not remove from file cabinet drawers, document cases, or folders.

    2. Do not turn containers upside down to empty or drain.

B. Separation of wet sheets

    1. Place a stack of polyester film on top of a stack of wet, unbound papers (or the first page of a bound volume).

2. Run gently with a bone folder–surface friction will cause the wet paper to adhere to the film.

3. Peel back the top sheet and place it on top of a piece of polyester web.

4. Remove the polyester film.

5. Place another sheet of polyester web on top of the wet sheet.

6. Repeat the entire process, separating the wet sheets one at a time and interleaving them with polyester web. (Materials may be frozen at this stage.)

7. Air dry the sheets (supported by the polyester web) by placing them on absorbent paper on tables or on top of closely spaced monofilament lines. Air in the room should be kept circulating, but fans should not blow directly on the materials.

8. The papers may be flattened when they are almost dry by placing them between two sheets of blotting paper (to remove excess moisture) and applying even pressure with weights.

VI. **Nonbook materials**

A. Photographic materials (prints, negatives, slides, film)

Do not expect to salvage color photographs, as the colored layers will separate and the dyes will fade quickly. However, if you wish to try, freeze them immediately, or transport them (see 2 below) to a photographic laboratory.

Photographic materials should not be allowed to dry out after they become wet as they will stick to their envelopes or to each other. Any attempt to separate them after they have dried together will result in damage to the emulsion or the image. Remove the materials from their protective enclosures and wash off any mud or dirt under cold, clean, running water.

The following options are available for salvaging photographic materials:

1. Air dry either flat or on lines of monofilament. (Plastic spring-type clothespins may be used to hang them on the line.)

2. If there are too many to air dry, they may be stored in cold water (65 degrees F or below–cold helps to preserve the emulsion). Ice may be added to the water, but **do not add dry ice or allow the materials to remain under water longer than three days.**

    Formaldehyde may be added to the water (15 milliliters to one liter) to help prevent the gelatin from swelling and softening. Black and white film could last three days in this solution before the emulsion begins to separate; color film could last 48 hours.

    Transport the materials (in sealed polyethylene bags inside plastic garbage pails) to a professional laboratory within 24 hours, if possible.

3. If time does not permit air drying, the materials may be frozen. As the emulsion may be damaged by the formation of ice crystals, freezing as quickly as possible is recommended (smaller ice crystals will cause less damage). Negatives should be separated before freezing as they tend to stick together when thawed.

4.   The Eastman Kodak Company provides free emergency service for cleaning and drying its own black and white roll microfilm. Contact Don Franklin in the Chicago lab (312-954-6000).

B.   Microforms

    1.   Silver halide microfilm

        a.   Keep under water (see V.A. 2 above).
        b.   Send to Kodak or a professional microprocessing laboratory.

    2.   Vessicular and diazo microfilm

        a.   Wash off mud or dirt under cold, clean running water.
        b.   Air dry or dry with cheesecloth.

    3.   Microfiche

        a.   Treat the same as silver halide microfilm.
        b.   Kodak will not treat microfiche, so send them to a professional microprocessing laboratory.

C.   Tapes (audio, video, computer) and floppy disks

Water is especially damaging to magnetic materials. The longer they have been wet, the greater the damage will be. Do not attempt to play any damaged tapes or disks, as they can damage the equipment on which they are being played. The following procedures are recommended if you wish to attempt to salvage tapes:

    1.   Break open the cassettes.

    2.   Wash in clean or distilled water.

3.   Air dry with cheesecloth.

D.   Sound recordings (disks)

Clean water probably will not damage sound recordings, but flood water carries silt, which will scratch the disk. Disks should be washed and dried with cheesecloth or a soft, lint-free cloth. Record jackets or paper protective sleeves should be discarded as they can trap moisture and may develop mold. Record jackets could be photocopied to preserve the information they contain.

VI.   **Mold**

Mold and mildew are interchangeable names for fungi. They can never be killed and can remain dormant for many years. Spores are always present in the air and will grow when the environment is warm and humid. Freezing will inhibit the growth of mold and is recommended if time does not permit immediate treatment.

A.   Mold can develop within 48 to 72 hours in an environment where the temperature is over 75 degrees F and the relative humidity is over 60 percent.

B.   Separate the affected materials to prevent spreading.

C.   If the materials are wet and mold is beginning to develop, interleave the volumes with papers impregnated with fungicide (see II.C.4).

D.   Keep the air circulating in the room.

E.   Mold is easier to remove when it is dry. Vacuum or brush it off and remove the spores from the area.

F.   Materials that will be fumigated should be removed from plastic crates, as plastic will absorb the fumigants. Fungicidal fogging should be done only by a professional chemist or conservator.

VII.   **DO NOT, UNDER ANY CIRCUMSTANCES:**

Enter an area until it has been declared safe.

Attempt to close an open book that is swollen.

Use mechanical presses on wet materials.

Attempt to separate books that are stuck together.

Write on wet paper.

Use bleaches, detergents, water-soluble fungicides, adhesive tapes (or adhesives of any kind), paper clips, or staples on wet materials.

Use colored paper of any kind during salvage and recovery operations.

Pack newly dried materials in boxes or leave them unattended for more than two days.

**FOR ASSISTANCE IN WRITING YOUR DISASTER PLAN
OR FOR HELP FOLLOWING A DISASTER, CALL
THE ILLINOIS STATE LIBRARY PRESERVATION OFFICE
(217)524-5866 (WEEKDAYS)
(217)546-2782 (ALL OTHER TIMES)**

Bibliography

Introduction: Preservation – the National Perspective

Council on Library Resources, Commission on Preservation and Access. *Brittle Books: Reports of the Committee on Preservation and Access.* Washington, D.C.: Council on Library Resources, 1986.

Darling, Pamela W. "Our Fragile Inheritance: The Challenge of Preserving Library Materials."*1978 ALA Yearbook.* Chicago: American Library Association, 1978, xxxi-xlii.

Lundeen, Gerald, ed. "Conservation of Library Materials." *Library Trends* 30, no. 2 (Fall 1981). (The entire 317-page issue is devoted to the topic of conservation.)

Morrow, Carolyn Clark, with Gay Walker. *The Preservation Challenge: A Guide to Conserving Library Materials.* White Plains, N.Y.: Knowledge Industry Publications, 1983.

Preservation of Library Materials. IFLA Publications 40/41. Edited by Merrily Smith. 2 vols. Munich: K.G. Saur Verlag, 1987.

Ritzenthaler, Mary Lynn. *Archives and Manuscripts: Conservation.* SAA Basic Manual Series. Chicago: Society of American Archivists, 1983.

Wilson, Alexander. *Library Policy for Preservation and Conservation in the European Community: Principles, Practices and the Contribution of New Information Technologies.* Commission of the European Communities, Directorate-General Telecommunications, Information Industries and

Innovation Publication, no. EUR 11563. Munich: K.G. Saur Verlag, 1988.

Preservation and Disaster Planning

Preservation Planning in Florida

Banks, Paul N. "Preservation of Library Materials." In *Encyclopedia of Library and Information Science*, edited by A. Kent, H. Lancour and J. E. Daily, Vol. 23. New York: Marcel Dekker, 1978, 180-222. A comprehensive overview of problems associated with and methods of preserving library materials.

Council on Library Resources. *Brittle Books: Reports of the Committee on Preservation and Access*. Washington, D.C.: Council on Library Resources, 1986. A brief overview of preservation issues addressed by the committee with emphasis on the worldwide problem of disintegrating books printed on acidic paper. Reports suggest approaches to preserving library and archival information.

DePew, John N. *A Library Media, and Archival Preservation Source Book*. Santa Barbara, Calif.: ABC-CLIO, October 1990. A compilation and explanation of problems and solutions in the preservation of book and paper, magnetic media, and film and photographic materials.

– – –. *Statewide Disaster Preparedness and Recovery Program for Florida Libraries*. Occasional Paper no. 185. Champaign, Ill.: University of Illinois, Graduate School of Library and Information Science, February 1989. A report describing six disaster preparedness workshops and the establishment of a disaster support network for academic and public libraries in Florida.

– – –. "Time is Running Out: An Investigation of the Preservation Needs of Florida Libraries; LSCA Title III Project Funded by the State Library of Florida." *FLASH* 9 (October 1989): 8-9. A brief discussion of the LSCA Title III project currently being conducted in Florida to determine the preservation needs and options of the state's academic and public libraries.

National Conservation Advisory Council (U.S.). Study Committee on Libraries and Archives. *Report of the Study Committee on Libraries and Archives: National Needs in Libraries and Archives Conservation*. Washington, D.C.: The Council, 1978. The National Conservation Advisory Council was established in 1973 as a national forum for cooperation and planning among institutions and cultural property in the U.S. This report was the first to identify and describe the preservation needs and problems of libraries and archives in the U.S. It concludes with seven recommendations for action.

New York Document Conservation Advisory Council. *Our Memory at Risk: Preserving New York's Unique Research Resources: A Report and Recommendations to the Citizens of New York.* Albany: New York State Education Department, 1988. One of the first reports by a state on the condition of archives, manuscripts, newspapers and documents held in institutions within its borders. It provides an overview of preservation problems, describes conditions in the state's repositories, and recommends actions to ensure the survival of cultural materials or the information they contain.

Preservation – Regional and Statewide Planning

Following is a brief list of recommended readings on regional and statewide planning developed by Lisa L. Fox. (See the preface.)

Bookmark 45, no. 3 (Spring 1987). Focus of this special theme issue is on preservation. Includes discussion of cooperative statewide programs in Illinois, New Jersey, and New York, along with SOLINET, ARL, and other organizations.

Commission on Preservation and Access. *Newsletter.* Excellent source of timely reports on cooperative national and international preservation activities. Particularly strong coverage of issues related to reformatting, bibliographic control, and research development.

Fox, Lisa L. "The SOLINET Preservation Program: Building a Preservation Network in the Southeast." *The New Library Scene* 7 (August 1988): 1, 5-9. An analytical description, focusing on efforts to build a distributed network of preservation responsibilities at the local, state, and regional levels in the Southeast.

Gwinn, Nancy E. "The Rise and Fall and the Rise of Cooperative Projects." *Library Resources and Technical Services* 29 (January/March 1985): 80-86. A good overview of the history of cooperative preservation of mirofilming projects in the U.S.

Hope for the Future: A Report on the Preservation of South Carolina's Paper-Based Records. Columbia, S.C.: Palmetto Archives, Libraries and Museums Council on Preservation, 1989. A report of the statewide preservation needs assessment project carried out in South Carolina, with an action agenda for developing leadership, educational programs, and funding sources to establish a decentralized preservation program for the state.

National Endowment for the Humanities, Office of Preservation. *Preservation Programs: Guidelines and Application Instructions*. (1990.) The *Guidelines* include a new funding category for cooperative statewide preservation planning, as well as continued funding of regional and institutional projects. Copies of funded proposals, available from the Office of Preservation, often offer useful models to prospective applicants.

New York Document Conservation Advisory Council. *Our Memory at Risk: Preserving New York's Unique Research Resources*. Albany: New York State Education Department, 1988. This book is a result of an intensive statewide project of needs assessment and consensus building led by the New York State Archives. It provides a rationale and plan of action for a concerted preservation effort focusing on archival materials.

Born in Fire: Arson, Emergency Actions, and Recovery of the Joliet Public Library

American Hospital Association Resource Center. *Library of the American Hospital Association, Asa S. Bacon Memorial and Hospital Literature Service Policy and Procedure Statement*, May 1987.

American Libraries 20, no. 11 (December 1989) 1022, 1025, 1026.

American Libraries 21, no. 2 (January 1990): 110.

Burgess, Dean. "The Library Has Blown Up!" *Library Journal* (1 October 1989).

"Central Library Fire." *Communicator* 19, no. 3-6 (March-June 1986). (Los Angeles County Public Library Newsletter.)

Chicago Area Disaster Response Resource File. Newberry Library, Chicago, Ill., 1988.

Clarke, Arthur C. *2010*. (New York: Granada Publishers, 1982).

Covey, Stephen R. *Seven Habits of Highly Effective People*. New York: Simon and Schuster, 1989.

DePew, John N. *Statewide Disaster Preparedness and Recovery Program for Florida Libraries*. Occasional Paper no. 185. Champaign, Ill.: University of Illinois, Graduate School of Library and Information Science, February 1989.

Disaster Preparedness and Recovery Plan for the Chicago Public Library, January 1989.

Gozzi, Cynthia I. "When the Earth Moved, So Did Technical Services." *ALCTS Newsletter* 1, no. 1 (1990): 1-2.

Illinois Library Materials Preservation Task Force. *The Preservation of Library and Archival Resources in Illinois: A Five-Year Plan of Action*. Springfield: Illinois State Library, April 1986.

Illinois State Library Preservation Office. *Basic Guidelines for Disaster Planning*. Springfield: Illinois State Library Preservation Office.

Lundquist, Eric G., *Salvage of Water Damaged Books, Documents, Micrographic and Magnetic Media*. San Francisco, Calif.: Document Reprocessors of San Francisco, 1986.

Murray, Toby. *Basic Guidelines for Disaster Planning in Oklahoma*. Oklahoma City: State Library of Oklahoma, 1989.

Myers, Gerald E. *Insurance Manual for Libraries*. Chicago: ALA, 1977.

Nudell, Mayer, and Norman Antokol. *The Handbook for Effective Emergency and Crisis Management*. Lexington, Mass.: Lexington Books, 1988.

Schaefer, George L. "Fire!" *Library Journal*, 85, no. 3 (1 February 1960): 504-5.

Schell, H. B. "Cornell Starts a Fire." *Library Journal* (1 October 1961): 3398-99.

Thigpen, Joe D. *Coping with Library Disasters*. Presented to the Inland Empire Libraries Disaster Response Network, Loma Linda University. 21 March 1988.

Waters, Peter. *Procedures for Salvage of Water Damaged Materials*. 2d ed. Washington: Library of Congress, 1979.

Young, Richard F., and Biblio Prep Films, Oakton, Va. *Library and Archival Disaster: Preparedness and Recovery*. Chicago: ALA, 1986 ($125.00, 21-minute video plus 16-page workbook: 0-8389-2085).

Pressures on the Process of Scholarly Exchange

Association of Research Libraries. *Report of the ARL Serials Prices Project.* Washington, D.C.: Association of Research Libraries, May 1989.

Association of Research Libraries. *Serials Prices and Research Libraries: Some Frequently Asked Questions.* Washington, D.C.: Association of Research Libraries, August 1988.

CRS Report for Congress. *Research Journal Prices – Trends and Problems,* 31 March 1988.

Dougherty, Richard M. "Turning the Serials Crisis to Our Advantage: An Opportunity for Leadership." *Library Administration and Management* 3, no. 2 (Spring 1989): 59-63.

Horowitz, Irving L. "Monopolization of Publishing and Crisis in Higher Education." *Academe* vol. 73, no. 6 (November/December 1987): 41-43.

Houbeck, Robert L., Jr. "If Present Trends Continue: Responding to Journal Price Increases." *Journal of Academic Librarianship* 13, no. 4 (September 1987): 214-20.

Kaufman, Paula. "A Crisis in Scholarly Publication – Serials Price Escalation and New Title Proliferation." *Information Issues* (Fall 1989): 1-4.

Lynden, Frederick C. "Prices of Foreign Library Materials: A Report." *College and Research Libraries* 49, no. 3 (May 1988): 217-31.

Selsky, Deborah. "Libraries Face Continued Price Increases of Books and Periodicals." *Library Journal* 114, no.15, (15 September 1989): 28.

The Role and Effectiveness of the Public Library

Conflicting Roles of the Public Library

Ballard, Thomas, H. *The Failure of Resource Sharing in Public Libraries and Alternative Strategies for Service.* Chicago: American Library Association, 1986.

Childers, Thomas, and Nancy Van House. *The Public Library Effectiveness Study: Final Report.* Philadelphia: Drexel University, 1989.

Honan, William H. "Say Goodbye to the Stuffed Elephants." *The New York Times Magazine,* 14 January 1990, 35-38.

McClure, Charles, Amy Owen, Douglas Zweizig, Mary Jo Lynch, and Nancy A. Van House. *Planning and Role Setting for Public Libraries*. Chicago: American Library Association, 1987.

Summers, F. William. "Alternatives to the Central Library." *Public Libraries* 23, no. 1 (Spring 1984): 4-7.

Winokur, Jon, comp. *The 1990 Daily Curmudgeon Calendar*. New York: New American Library, 1989.

The Effectiveness of the Public Library

Cameron, Kim S. "Study of Organizational Effectiveness and Its Predictors." *Management Science* 32 (1986): 87-112.

Childers, Thomas, and Nancy A. Van House. "The Grail of Goodness: The Effective Public Library." *Library Journal* 114, no. 16 (1 October 1989): 44-49.

Childers, Thomas, and Nancy A. Van House. *The Public Library Effectiveness Study: Final Report*. Philadelphia: Drexel University College of Information Studies, 1989.

Heskett, James L. "Lessons in the Service Sector." *Harvard Business Review* 65, no. 2 (March-April 1987): 118-25.

Jobson, J. D., and Rodney Schneck. "Constituent Views of Organizational Effectiveness: Evidence from Police Organizations." *Academy of Management Journal* 25 (1982): 25-46.

Prottas, Jeffrey Mandich. "The Cost of Free Service: Organizational Impediments to Access to Public Services." *Public Administration Review* 41, no. 5 (September/October 1981): 526-34.

Samuel Lazerow Memorial Lecture

The National Legislative Agenda

Brown, George. "National Policy Concerns." *Libraries and the Information Economy in California: A Conference Sponsored by the California State Library*. Edited by Robert M. Hayes. Los Angeles: A GSLIS/UCLA Publication, 1985, 53-78.

"California: The Next Twenty Years. Twentieth Anniversary Issue. Fifteen Californians Peer into the Future for a Look at Their Home State's Next 20 Years." *California Journal*, January 1990.

Molz, R. Kathleen. *The Federal Roles in Support of Public Library Services: An Overview*. Prepared for the Federal Roles in Support of Public Library Services Project. Chicago: American Library Association, 1990.

"One Nation, 250 Million Individuals, Public Library Services for a Diverse People: The Roles of the Federal Government. Twenty-four library leaders ask you to read this document – and react to it – at Midwinter." *American Libraries* 20, no. 11 (December 1989): 1104 ff.

Payne, Judith, *Public Libraries Face California's Ethnic and Racial Diversity*. Prepared for the Stanford University Libraries with a grant from the California State Library. Santa Monica, Calif.: The RAND Corporation, 1988.

A State of Change: California's Ethnic Future and Libraries. Conference and Awareness Forum Proceedings, 1988. Edited by Nora Jacob, Project Coordinator. Presented by the Planning Group for "A State of Change." Sacramento: California State Library Foundation, 1988.

Strong, Gary E. "Impact of the Federal Government on State Library Services." *State Library Services and Issues: Facing Future Challenges*. Edited by Charles R. McClure. Norwood, New Jersey: Ablex Publishing Corporation, 1986, 50-61.

The Federal and State Legislative Agenda

American Library Association. *ALA Federal Legislative Policy*. Chicago: ALA, 1987.

American Library Association. *Less Access to Less Information, by and about the U.S. Government: A 1985-1989 Chronology*. Washington: ALA, 1989.

American Library Association. *Legislative Report of the ALA Washington Office January-December 1989*. Chicago: ALA, 1989.

Association of Specialized and Cooperative Library Agencies, ALA. Multitype Library Cooperation Section. Legislation Committee. *Multitype Library Cooperation, State Laws and Regulations: An Annotated Checklist*. Chicago: ASCLA/ALA, 1983.

Cooke, Eileen C. "Capitol Hill Perspective." *Libraries and Political Process*, Occasional Papers of the Minnesota Library Association, no. 1. Minnesota: MLA, 1989, 22-26.

An Evaluation of Title I of the Library Services and Construction Act. Final Report prepared for Office of Program Evaluation, U.S. Department of Education, January 1981.

Federal Funding Alternatives. National Commission on Libraries and Information Science, October 1979.

Improving State Aid to Public Libraries. Report prepared for the Urban Libraries Council. Washington, D.C.: National Commission on Libraries and Information Science, 1977.

Ladenson, A. D. "Essential Now-Direct State Aid to Public Libraries." *Library Journal* 104, no. 7 (1 April 1979): 801-5.

Owens, Major R. "Federal and State Library Legislation: A United Strategy." *Library Journal* 102, no. 9 (1 May 1977): 988-90.